Randy Wood

To Lloyd

Hope you like the tote!

Randy

THE CHARLES K. WOLFE MUSIC SERIES

Ted Olson, Series Editor

Randy Wood

THE LORE OF THE LUTHIER

— Daniel Wile —

THE UNIVERSITY OF TENNESSEE PRESS

KNOXVILLE

The Charles K. Wolfe Music Series was launched in honor of the
late Charles K. Wolfe (1943–2006), whose pioneering work in the study of
American vernacular music brought a deepened understanding of a wide range
of American music to a worldwide audience. In recognition of Dr. Wolfe's
approach to music scholarship, the series will include books that investigate
genres of folk and popular music as broadly as possible.

Copyright © 2020 by The University of Tennessee Press / Knoxville.
All Rights Reserved. Manufactured in the United States of America.

First Edition.

Library of Congress Cataloging-in-Publication Data
Names: Wile, Daniel, 1981– author.
Title: Randy Wood : the lore of the luthier / Daniel Wile.
Description: First edition. | Knoxville : The University of Tennessee Press, 2020. |
Series: The Charles K. Wolfe music series |
Includes bibliographical references and index. |
Summary: "In the 1960s and 1970s, Randy Wood was one of the pioneers in the
vintage instrument industry. He brought cherished pre-WWII instruments back to
life, many of which owners and buyers thought could not be repaired. He crafted
his own instruments as well and was operating in Nashville during the resurgence
of country music and the rapid evolution of the music industry into a business
juggernaut. All the while Wood's instruments collectively found their way into the
hands of some of country music and the music industry's more renowned artists.
Daniel Wile presents Wood as an important component of the overall history of
country music in Nashville and beyond, and presents his craftsmanship of stringed
instruments as functional, musical works of art."—Provided by publisher.
Identifiers: LCCN 2020003773 (print) | LCCN 2020003774 (ebook) |
ISBN 9781621905530 (paperback) | ISBN 9781621905547 (adobe pdf)
Subjects: LCSH: Wood, Randy (Luthier) | Luthiers—United States—
Biography. | Guitar makers—United States—Biography.
Classification: LCC ML424.W66 W55 2020 (print) | LCC ML424.W66 (ebook) |
DDC 787.19092 [B]—dc23
LC record available at https://lccn.loc.gov/2020003773
LC ebook record available at https://lccn.loc.gov/2020003774

TO ANNA

CONTENTS

ILLUSTRATIONS

Fingerboard with Elvis Inlay

Detail of Elvis Inlay

Old Time Picking Parlor Music Store

Randy Wood

Old Time Picking Parlor Jam Session

Old Time Picking Parlor Workshop

Randy in Old Time Picking Parlor Workshop

Randy Filing a Guitar Neck

Guitar Clamped While Glue Dries

Randy Inspecting a Guitar

Coley Coleman and Randy Wood

Charlie Collins and Norman Blake

"Bashful Brother Oswald" Kirby,
Charlie Collins, and Roy Acuff

Charlie Collins and "Bashful Brother Oswald" Kirby

Vassar Clements and Lawrence Lee White

The Whites with Norman Blake, Jack Hicks,
Terry Dearborn, and Mark O'Connor

Hatch Show Print for Whites Concert

Informal Jamming in the Picking Parlor

Country Gazette (Alan Munde, Dave Ferguson [?],
Roger Bush, and Roland White)

FOREWORD

Long before Nashville was nicknamed "Guitar Town" (the CB handle for the city, borrowed by Steve Earle for the title of his mid-1980s hit song) —around the time Nashville was just a hardscrabble frontier community—Beethoven in the Old World referred to that particular musical instrument as "a veritable orchestra unto itself." Granted his many obligations to crank out immortal, beloved classical compositions for Viennese aristocrats, Beethoven was a folk revivalist at heart, being, for instance, an enthusiast of instruments associated with certain national groups, including the Italian mandolin and the Spanish guitar. The vaunted composer understood that the latter instrument—whether found in folk, popular, or elite environments—was singularly suited to be played solo. But he also knew that not all guitars were created equal—that the relative loudness, richness, and purity of tone in a given instrument depended upon the materials and craftsmanship with which it was built.

Through most of the last century and certainly in this one, countless American roots musicians have likewise lauded the guitar for its unique ability to build its own sonic castles (or, perhaps more apt for the iconography of rural America, sonic cabins). By the 1940s when the commercial country music industry was consolidated in Nashville, the guitar was the go-to instrument for accompanying songs in countless recordings and live performances. Then as bluegrass took off from the Grand Ole Opry stage, other instruments in various combinations competed for a share of Nashville's soundscape. And someone needed to make all those instruments and to keep them sounding at their best.

As Beethoven's mandolin compositions (a few of which have entered the repertoire of bluegrass mandolinists) and the recordings of Bill Monroe equally demonstrate, vernacular music—though accessible to people from all walks of life—reaches its potential as art when emanating from the throats or hands of skilled practitioners who perform that music within communities that value such art. Whereas vocals are created by God-given vocal cords, tunes or song accompaniments depend upon the manipulation of manmade instruments. With that realization in mind, it is perhaps not entirely hyperbole to say that the essential figures in any music culture are the Creator and the Luthier. Ample credit has been granted to the former (the common explanation for a person's vocal magnificence is the person "has God-given talent"), yet luthiers—makers of stringed instruments—are generally overlooked, taken for granted. Too often, music fans praise skilled instrumentalists for their virtuosity with nary a nod to the luthiers who melded raw materials together by hand to shape the vessels that can transport the listener into the sublime. Of course, musicians deserve to be lauded for learning and mastering their instruments . . . but in the cosmos of music, luthiers are gods; and during Nashville's music renaissance of the 1970s many musicians and fans-in-the-know deemed one of the city's luthiers as deserving a place in the pantheon: Randy Wood.

As if destined to embody his last name, this living legend has built countless instruments out of many types of wood. (Daniel Wile, the author of this biography, reminds us that "the luthier's fundamental challenge" is "coercing a tree to sing.") Based in Nashville in the 1970s, Wood built sought-after guitars and other stringed instruments—mandolins, ukuleles, and banjos—for professional musicians as well as for recreational pickers. And Wood could reanimate other people's damaged instruments, restoring to working order everything from treasured pre–World War II classics to manufacturer knock-offs. To Nashville's music community during that period, though, Wood was more than an instrument builder/repairer par excellence: he was simultaneously a gatekeeper. His operation of the Old Time Picking Parlor, a revered music performance venue as humble and accessible (reflecting Wood's character) as Ryman Auditorium and the Opry House were both grand and grandiloquent.

As is the general fate of luthiers (Guy Clark was the exception, but his fame came mostly from performing and songwriting), Wood is not a household name. Hopefully Wile's book will bring broader recognition by transporting readers into Wood's world. This book revisits Wood's roles in Nashville and traces his subsequent return to his roots in Georgia, where he continues to serve music communities in the parallel roles he has long balanced: building and repairing instruments (presently in his Bloomingdale, Georgia, store/workshop) and hosting music performances (now in his new venue, Randy's Picking Parlor). People continue to seek Wood out because he is a music master with a rare understanding of the instruments that make music possible. Randy Wood may have moved many miles from Nashville, but wherever he is, *that* place is "Guitar Town."

Ted Olson
East Tennessee State University

ACKNOWLEDGMENTS

Randy Wood has a way of imparting lessons without appearing to do any teaching. I should not have been surprised that working on a project with and about Randy would teach me as much about life and about myself as it would about him. I have spent the last few years collecting recorded conversations with people whose lives were enriched by their friendship with Randy. Yet I look back on this project with a sense of awe over the personal growth I experienced between the starting and finish lines. I also look back with much gratitude. Along the way, many great people offered enormous help on this fulfilling journey.

My list of people to thank must begin with Randy. When I pitched the idea of a biography to him back in 2010, he must have wondered why I thought I was qualified to write a book about him. He would have been right to wonder. Nevertheless, he immediately agreed to my idea and then patiently spent many of his precious late-night working hours in his shop with me so I could pepper him with questions about his life. Then, he calmly talked through countless phone calls to fill in gaps in the story.

Even if I had not embarked on writing this book, I would still owe many thanks to Randy. At his establishment, I learned the joy of playing music with others. But I learned more than just how to play. Randy gave me a place where I could be immersed in the activity. I learned about the history of and the people behind the music. The Dobro—my instrument of choice—may have been the seed from which those experiences sprouted, but Randy, you provided the fertile soil.

Irene and Renee, you also put up with my frequent visits to your home so I could interview Randy. Irene, you often bore the challenging task of keeping order in the shop so that the rest of us could enjoy peaceful surroundings with Randy. During my interviews, it became clear that most of

Randy's admirers recognize that without your unwavering support, much of his work would have been impossible.

This book would remain just a dream without the support Thomas Wells at the University of Tennessee Press. Thomas, you believed in this project and helped me turn an eight-year-old idea into a beautiful finished product. Thank you to everyone at the University of Tennessee Press for helping me cross the finish line.

You likely would not be reading about Randy Wood's career were it not for the influence of George Gruhn and Tut Taylor, the "G" and the "T" in GTR, respectively. I consider myself fortunate to have spent a few hours with each of them. George, your pursuit of excellence is evident to anyone who loves vintage instruments. You renewed my conviction that excellence is built upon attention to detail. Tut, you welcomed a stranger into your home and had me spellbound with your stories of the fun you had in Nashville. After our interview, I was thrilled to jam with you on a few Dobro tunes. I speak for the Dobro community when I say you are and will be missed.

I had the good fortune of talking with many people who have worked alongside Randy. Scott Kinsey, thank you for shedding light on Randy's quieter years on Isle of Hope. Wayne Henderson, thank you for your stories of Randy's pragmatism. Chris Camp, thank you for a very meaty phone interview. I have listened to that recording enough times to recognize your voice anywhere! Danny Ferrington, one of the highlights of this entire process was spending an afternoon hanging out in your Santa Monica shop. Your encouragement of what I was doing came at a time when I sorely needed it. You also shared some amazing photographs. J. T. Gray, thank you for talking with me during a quiet afternoon in the Station Inn. It was magical hearing you share memories of the Old Time Picking Parlor, and I became aware we were sitting in a place that is spawning memories for a new generation of Nashvillians.

Some of Randy's closest friends gave me a glimpse into his early years. Curtis Burch, it was a treat to meet an important figure in Randy's life who also happens to be a giant in the Dobro world. Thank you to Raymond Huffmaster. Who knew that one of Randy's best friends lives only a few miles from where I grew up and now live? It seems I often find Randy's fingerprints where I least expect them.

Fellow luthiers and instrument gurus gave me context for assessing Randy's place in the instrument world. Steve Gilchrist, thank you for further validating my belief that Randy's story needs to be told. To hear such a renowned luthier speak so highly of Randy strengthened my resolve. John Hedgecoth, thank you for the warmth you showed when you welcomed me into your home. Roger Siminoff, you provided great insights on Randy's career. You also wrote a wonderfully informative article about Lloyd Loar's life. Tony Williamson, you were one of my first interviews, and you gave me a broad foundation of mandolin history to build upon. Darryl and Bobby Wolfe, thank you for sharing your expertise on F-5 mandolins. Roger Campbell, I was fortunate to see you twice—in Nashville and Meridian. I am excited to finally share the finished product that you have so eagerly anticipated.

I am grateful to have met many musicians who are experienced players of Randy's instruments. I would like to thank a few here. Roland White, you explained how a professional musician thinks about the tools of his trade. Red Henry, you have been gracious with stories and photos; I am always drawn to fellow aviators. Mike Compton, you reminded me that when someone makes us feel at home when in a strange new place, as Randy did when you moved to Nashville, the impact can be enormous.

Thank you to the many music industry professionals who shed light on the Picking Parlor days. Charlie Collins, your warmth and humility showed me why you were such a beloved member of the Picking Parlor regulars. I learned that these qualities, when lived genuinely, make lasting impressions on those around us. Bil VornDick, you helped create some of my favorite albums, and I thank you for your perspective on the Picking Parlor's place in the Nashville scene. John McEuen, you showed me how even the biggest musical talents can turn into kids when talking about their heroes. Buck White, thank you for your stories of the Picking Parlor while we met for breakfast. You even showed me how to charm a waitress. Ed Foote, thank you for responding to my classified ad asking for stories of the Picking Parlor. Your observation of the sharpness of Randy's carving knives made me appreciate how the smallest details of our behavior often speak the loudest.

This book would not be what it is today without the generous contribution of beautiful photographs of Randy's work and his surroundings. J. D. Sloan, thank you for sharing such beautiful photos that captured the essence of the Picking Parlor. Thank you also for teaching me to search for the questions, not the answers. Jeffrey Marren and Laura Pickett at Graceland, you helped me track down stunning photos of Randy's work on Elvis's guitar. Many thanks go to Dan Loftin, Jake Jacobson, Geoff Winningham, Richard Leo Johnson, Bobby Whitlock, and CoCo Carmel for the beautiful photography, as well.

I had no idea what I had bitten off when I decided to sink my teeth into a book project. There were many times of despair when there was no finish line in sight. But several people provided welcome illumination and inspiration. Pat Ahrens, at the beginning of this journey, you encouraged me to believe that I could accomplish this daunting project. You have an infectious enthusiasm for bluegrass! When I moved from Savannah to Mississippi, I was concerned that this partially-written book might die on the vine. I was fortunate to find several writers who helped me rekindle my energy to keep going. Richelle Putnam lifted my spirits and provided opportunities for me to practice my writing. When I was at a particularly low point, not knowing how to convert what was essentially a long term paper into a book, Steve Owen was a godsend. Steve, you put new wind in my sails, patiently reviewing my drafts and discussing them with me over your dining room table. You helped me believe I could do this. Dennis Satterlee, fellow regular at the Randy Wood weekend jams, I was inspired by your biography of Red Allen and thought perhaps I, too, could write a book. Thank you for the wisdom, guidance, encouragement, and review of my drafts.

Speaking of people I met at Randy's, I extend a big thank you to the weekend jam group. All of you nurtured this struggling Dobro player and welcomed me into the fold. In particular, thank you to Chuck "Fatt Lytr" Broom. Had you not welcomed me so enthusiastically during my first visit to Randy's, I might have been too intimidated to ever make a second trip. George Hicks, thank you for your mentorship and friendship. You taught me that it is much more rewarding to dive head-first into the deep end of a hobby rather than splash around in the shallow end.

My family has provided tremendous support through this endeavor. I am sure they all were puzzled when I announced that I intended to write a book. Thank you to my parents. Long before it ever looked like this book would become a reality, you took me seriously when I talked about this project. Hailey, you have always encouraged me to take a bigger step than I thought I was capable of taking. To my loving and patient wife, Anna, thank you for enduring all those weekends when I practically chained myself to my computer, saying, "I need to work on this book!" I hope I can provide as much support for your goals as you have provided for my goals.

Despite all the help I have received along the way, the act of writing is ultimately a singular process. The words—and any errors—in this book are mine.

Daniel Wile

May 2019

PROLOGUE

When Elvis Presley took the stage with his guitar at the *Aloha from Hawaii* concert, millions of television viewers saw Randy Wood's work. When Eric Clapton played slide guitar on his Grammy-winning *Unplugged* album, his fingers glided over Randy's inlay creation. The list of Wood's clients reads like a music hall of fame roster: Johnny Cash, Chet Atkins, Emmylou Harris, Billy Gibbons, Bill Monroe, Keith Richards, Roy Acuff, Ricky Skaggs, and Hank Williams Jr. Randy is known as the instrument repairman to the stars. Yet he is humble, unassuming, and unfazed by the presence of celebrities. His life's work has been devoted to building and repairing stringed instruments. While at work, he has opened his shop doors to let friends and strangers come in, visit, pick a little, and build community. What started simply as a quest to look forward to waking up each morning has turned into a career that has shaped a generation of musicians, professional and amateur alike.

Randy moved to Nashville in the early 1970s to be the instrument repairman—the luthier—for a new venture formed with friends and theretofore amateur instrument dealers Tut Taylor and George Gruhn. The new venture was dubbed GTR and was one of the first instrument stores in the United States dealing in vintage stringed instruments. Located behind the Ryman Auditorium, GTR became a popular destination for performers on rehearsal breaks and amateur pickers eager to rub shoulders with the greats. GTR became Gruhn Guitars, known today as the mecca of the vintage instrument world.

Randy and Tut left GTR and opened the Old Time Picking Parlor several blocks away on Nashville's Second Avenue. While GTR sought to be the purveyor of vintage instruments, the Picking Parlor appealed to a broader population of music enthusiasts. Within its wood-paneled walls, Wood and Taylor created a magical trifecta—a music store, a repair workshop, and a performance space. When bluegrass was enjoying a swell in popularity prompted by the banjo sounds in *The Beverly Hillbillies* and *Bonnie and Clyde*, the Old Time Picking Parlor was one of the top venues for bluegrass music in Nashville. The stars came into the Picking Parlor, as they did at GTR, during daytime respites from *Opry* rehearsals seeking repairs on their instruments or a few hours of jamming. Weekend pickers relished the chance to jam with their heroes. In the corners of his second-floor repair shop, Randy quietly held court over his apprentices, setting the example for humility and open-mindedness that permeated the Picking Parlor's culture. That culture left an indelible mark in the memories of a generation of Picking Parlor visitors.

In 1978 Randy returned to his native Georgia low country to escape the bustle of Nashville and devote more time to his original love of woodworking. However, his fans and devotees continued to seek his repair expertise and prompted Randy, once again, to open a commercial repair shop, this time in Bloomingdale, Georgia. Characteristically, this shop is more than a place where Randy trades and repairs instruments; it is a hub for bluegrass music activity throughout the Southeast.

It was at his Bloomingdale compound that I discovered Randy Wood one weekend in 2005 while on a mission to buy a Dobro, a brand of slide guitar that is somewhat obscure outside of bluegrass circles. I had been enchanted by the sounds of the instrument in the hands of Jerry Douglas, who played on some Alison Krauss CDs I had borrowed. Living in Savannah, Georgia, at the time, I scoured the local music stores for a Dobro but had no luck. Finally, one store clerk suggested I check out Randy's shop in nearby Bloomingdale. The following Saturday I made the twenty-minute westward drive to Bloomingdale to check out Randy Wood Guitars.

Even from the small parking lot I noticed the place had a pulse. In fact, it was audible, as the rhythmic thumping of an upright bass emanated from the rustic storefront. The front door squeaked as I entered, and a cowbell dangling from the inside handle announced my arrival. Guitars lined the walls of the small carpeted room. To my left, a clerk stood behind a lighted display case. Straight ahead, the music store opened to another merchandise room. From there, the sounds from that bass, plus a banjo, mandolin, and guitar, flowed throughout the shop as a group of men sat in a circle of metal folding chairs, playing their instruments. Through a side doorway to the back room where the jam was taking place, I could see a workshop aglow in fluorescent light. There were workbenches and tables and not a clear square inch on any of them. On one table, instruments in various stages of construction floated on top of a sea of old magazines and catalogs. The walls were lined with tool cabinets, shelves of books, CDs, and DVDs, guitar tops turned backward to expose the bracing underneath, and a wire string with violins hanging by the scrolls. A large flat screen television played a black-and-white cowboy movie.

Several men scurried around the workshop, but I easily spotted the store owner. He had a gravitas I could sense. He moved slowly and did not talk much. He was casual, wearing what I would later realize is his standard uniform: Hawaiian shirt untucked, draping over his belly; shorts; flip-flops; and a front shirt pocket bulging with pens, pencils, scales, screwdrivers, and business cards. He wore elegant, wire-rimmed reading glasses perched on his pointed nose. His thinning gray hair was combed neatly from front to back. He exuded a calm assuredness. This man did not have to announce that the name on the sign out front was his. I was intimidated by Randy at first glance. With his quiet demeanor, he did not exactly go out of his way to invite me in. I was downright scared to walk through the doorway into the workshop for fear that the jamming musicians might be secretly guarding the entrance, and my intrusion would bring the jam to a screeching halt.

As I stepped back from the workshop door and looked around the retail space, I noticed walls filled with photographs of Randy Wood with people who looked famous but were as yet unrecognizable to me, a neophyte bluegrass fan. However, one framed photo caught my eye. It showed Randy staring back at the camera calmly while two smiling men flanked him on either side. I recognized these performers; they were both members of Alison Krauss's band, Union Station. One was Ron Block and the other was Jerry Douglas, the man whose music had inspired my quest that brought me to Randy's shop in the first place. I felt I had stumbled upon something special here. Later I would learn to identify the other faces in the photographs scattered around the walls of Randy Wood Guitars. Those pictures of Johnny Cash, Hank Williams Jr., Norman Blake, Tony Rice, Earl Scruggs, and Vassar Clements were portraits of giants of their genres. I would also learn they were standing with a giant in the world of musical instruments.

I bought a beginner Dobro and made a habit of driving out to Bloomingdale to join the Saturday afternoon jams. As I began to feel more comfortable in the place, I mustered the courage to walk into the workshop and get to know Randy. It was not long before I considered him a friend, as did all of the weekend pickers. The more I watched musicians coming in and out of the store, the more I realized Randy had a lot of friends. Always willing to visit, Randy, in his syrupy slow drawl, would tell stories from his career spent around music's most recognizable names, all the while sitting in a swivel chair with a carving knife in one hand and an unfinished mandolin back in the other.

Today new customers may look to Randy for help repairing an instrument, but his impact on the music world reaches far beyond repaired guitar frets and warped necks. He has created spaces where music enthusiasts of all stripes can hang out, surrounded by people who speak their language. Randy sets the example for how to behave. All people in the shop are to be treated as friends, whether they have sold a million albums or just picked up a guitar for the first time. Careers have been launched from the networking Randy has facilitated. Lifelong relationships took root. Thanks to the weekend jams I regularly attended at Randy's, the Dobro has become more than an inanimate curiosity piece. It has been my ticket to a world rich with friendships and inspiring encounters with my musical heroes. Randy's great achievement is his wide circle of friends who can relate to my experience.

Randy is too understated to write a book about himself, and after several years of hanging out in his shop and hearing his stories, I began thinking, "Somebody needs to write a book about this guy." At some point I thought just maybe I could be that somebody. At first I assumed I would develop a series of stories around notable musicians influenced by Randy's work. But after many interviews with important people in Randy's life and many more conversations with Randy in his workshop during quiet, late-night sessions, I realized my focus was in the wrong direction. Sure, star power of Randy's customer base makes for great stories, but I was naïve to assume that a story of Randy's life needed to be propped up by the fragile veneer of celebrity associations. Randy is remarkable because the celebrities revere him.

Randy's is a story of a luthier who has quietly influenced bluegrass and country music. Randy's own stories and the accounts from family and friends are entertaining in themselves. Assembled together, they reveal an inspiring theme: a humble man with passion for his craft, a genuine affection for people, and the courage to follow his heart can leave an indelible mark on the world.

THE LUTHIER'S CHALLENGE

*The heavier you build it, the less sound you're going to get. The
lighter you build it, the more chance there is that it's going to
fly apart. So, you've got to find that one little happy place.*

———————

TONY WILLIAMSON

What exactly is a luthier? The term sounds archaic, as though it belongs to
someone out of a Charles Dickens novel, working by the flickering light of
a crackling fire. The word seems quaint for someone as rugged as Randy
Wood. But, for more than half a century, Randy has earned his place as
one of the most respected American luthiers. A luthier builds and repairs
stringed instruments. Most of Randy's work can be seen in mandolins,
guitars, and banjos, but a visitor to his shop might also see upright basses
and violins or other exotic breeds of stringed instruments lying on work
benches. Although these instruments vary in size and shape, they pose
similar challenges to the luthier who builds or repairs them. The best instruments are marvels of engineering, acoustics, and artistry. Lutherie
requires a mastery of all three.

The lines between these disciplines blur for Randy. Lutherie is a natural expression of his sensibilities, irrespective of academic categorization.
Years of whittling, carving, and shaping wood—and a few collapsed instrument tops in the early years—have honed his judgment of structural
integrity. Randy's multitude of musician clients have guided the development of his ear via a valuable closed-loop feedback system; Randy sends
instruments into the world, and the players report back with what sounds
good on stage and in the studio. And the artistic demands of lutherie

appeal to Randy's natural zeal for craftsmanship. Indeed, one of the great ironies in Randy's life is that this Georgia farm boy, with massive hands and pickle fingers, is capable of exquisite, intricate artistic expression, be it with pencil on paper or mother-of-pearl on ebony.

The marriage of engineering, acoustics, and artistry is evident from an instrument's headstock to its endpin. The headstock provides space where tuning pegs anchor one end of the strings to the instrument. One of the few pieces of machinery on an acoustic instrument, the geared tuning pegs multiply the torque that a human hand can exert as the player adjusts the string tension to achieve a pleasing pitch. The angle of the headstock is important. Many guitars and mandolins exhibit headstocks sloping down from the plane of the fretboard. The luthier must carefully control this angle—too shallow and the strings will not seat firmly enough in the nut, too steep and the strings will dig too much. While the headstock serves a functional purpose, it is also prominent real estate for the builder's logo. Randy Wood designed a logo early in his career, and it has graced the headstocks of his instruments ever since. It is a vintage western *W*, graced by an interlaced *R* on each outer leg of the *W*.

Between an instrument's headstock and body, the neck demands particular care from the luthier. The back of the neck must be smooth and curved to be comfortable in the hands of the player. It must be narrow enough to accommodate small hands, but it must also be stout enough to handle the considerable forces on it. For a six-string guitar, the total tensile force in the strings may exceed 150 pounds. As long as that instrument stays in tune, the neck must be strong enough to resist this unrelenting compression reacting to the string tension. Compounding the problem is the height of the strings above the fretboard. They must be high enough above the frets and body to avoid touching the frets and buzzing when strummed. But a bent neck can result from too much offset between the tensile force exerted by the strings and the compressive reaction carried by the neck and body. Even a slight bend widens the gap between the strings and the higher frets, making the guitar more difficult to play. Randy turned this problem into an opportunity. Many frustrated guitar owners assumed their instrument was useless once the structural connection between the neck and body distorted beyond the point of playability. But Randy was an early adopter of the process to introduce heat into the joint between the neck and body, loosening the glue securing the dovetail joint. This allows him to remove the neck and reshape the angle of the mating face before reassembling the neck to the body. Neck resets have revived countless instruments.

Banjos, with their light-gauge strings, are not as vulnerable to neck distortion, but Randy has still spent considerable time on banjo necks. Rather than resetting dovetail joints, Randy's early banjo work focused on carving exquisite textured patterns in the base of the necks. His decorative embellishment of banjo necks attracted a crowd of customers, opening his eyes to the possibility that he could work on instruments for a living.

The fretboard glued on top of an instrument's neck is often a canvas for artistic expression by a luthier, but its design demands great mathematical precision as well. Much of Randy Wood's reputation is based on the beautiful mother-of-pearl inlays that he has placed in the fretboards of guitars belonging to some of music's biggest names. However, the primary job of the fretboard is to provide a place for a player's fingers to accurately note the strings. The spacing between each fret on a fretboard shrinks as one moves from the nut to the bridge, the distance diminishing according to a strict geometric ratio. Most luthiers are not actually working out the math on every instrument; they use templates. But the discerning ear can hear the incorrect pitch of an improperly spaced fret.

Stretched above the neck and fingerboard are the strings of an instrument. The strings are frequency generators responsible for starting the chain reaction leading to the ultimate tone of the instrument. When plucked, the strings oscillate back and forth and transmit oscillations through the bridge into the body, which, in turn, excites the air inside the body cavity to pulsate. The pulsing air waves transmit the sound to a listener's ears. It is tempting to assume the strings are the key to the tone of a stringed instrument. But anyone who has ever strummed an unplugged solid-body electric guitar knows the sound of the strings alone does not carry far. By contrast, unamplified acoustic guitars and mandolins, in the right hands, can fill a theater with rich music.

While the strings are important factors determining a stringed instrument's tone, the body's role is much more significant. The body of any

instrument can present the greatest tests of a luthier's skill. The significant forces imposed by the strings must be corralled while minimizing
the weight of materials in the body, since weight can affect the acoustics
of the piece. The acoustical considerations make the structural challenges
seem elementary.

The resonant frequency of any oscillating object depends on the ratio of
its stiffness to its mass. The higher the stiffness, the higher the frequency
at which it will resonate. A tight guitar string, when struck, will produce a
higher pitch than the same string under less tension. Conversely, the more
massive the object, the lower its natural frequency is. For example, the low
strings on a guitar are wound; the winding adds weight without adding
stiffness, therefore producing a low pitch in the plucked string.

The same principles relating resonant frequency to stiffness and mass
apply to the tops and backs of guitars and mandolins. Resonant frequencies dance and play across a guitar top like ballerinas on a stage. Low
notes respond to the big, wide, low-stiffness regions while the higher frequencies find their way to the areas with more reinforcement. On a typical
steel-stringed guitar, the top is not just a flat piece of wood. Inside, it is
braced with stiffeners in roughly X-patterns. The placement of these stiffeners is critical, defining which areas are best suited for the frequencies
scurrying around the top after they have made their way from the strings
and bridge. For the luthier, even the shape of these stiffeners becomes the
subject of intense study. He carves a corner here, shaves an edge there,
striving for that ideal balance of stiffness and mass.

Mandolins have less internal bracing, but luthiers strike the stiffness-
mass balance through a technique called graduation. Originally used by
violin makers hundreds of years ago, graduation is a process of carving the
insides of the top and back to vary the thickness across the pieces, achieving the proper topography from which a range of pleasant-sounding frequencies can resonate.

Mandolinist Tony Williamson aptly describes the challenge of striking
the balance between structural integrity of an instrument and its tonal
quality. "There's a structural element to the design of a musical instrument that has to adhere to the laws of physics. There's a lot of string tension there, and you've got to support it. But, the more you support it, the

less the box can vibrate. In other words, the heavier you build it, the less sound you're going to get. The lighter you build it, the more chance there is that it's going to fly apart. So, you've got to find that one little happy place. And, sometimes, that's like a thirty-second of an inch, the difference between sounding good and falling apart. Randy's the master of that—the horse sense of instrument-making." How does a luthier develop that sense?

In Randy's case, curiosity and experience have guided his journey to the mastery of construction. Randy's instruments have found their way into the hands of the greats, but he has also seen some of his early paper-thin mandolin tops collapse under the force of the strings. He had friends who owned some of the most sought-after Lloyd Loar era Gibson mandolins, and he has been able to study those instruments, measuring the dimensions and the thickness profile of the tops and backs to guide his own instrument designs. Randy also learned vicariously through his many apprentices who have climbed the lutherie learning curve under Randy's tutelage.

Of course, the end product resulting from all of this work has to look pleasing to the eye. Instruments are rightfully viewed by many as works of art. And their aesthetic beauty *should* be inspiring to the musician. It is not the rational, analytical side of the brain that is drawn to make music; it is the creative, artistic side. Even the structural joints of the body are not immune from embellishment. Some of the most valuable Martin guitars exhibit binding with a fishbone or "herringbone" pattern so distinctive that people know them as herringbone guitars. And even the smooth, clear coating over the gradient colors of a sunburst finish can captivate potential buyers. When a musician gets guitar fever, it is often the aesthetics of an instrument, not the science behind it, prompting the ailment.

What all these elements of lutherie share is the demand of the luthier to have intimate knowledge of wood, the fundamental material in the construction. Many observers have noted the irony of Randy Wood's last name being synonymous with the material with which he has plied his trade. Randy, who grew up on a farm, can hardly recall a time in his life when he was *not* working with wood. He became intimately familiar with the stuff from an early age. How it feels to carve, the tightness of the grain, the way the light reflects off its smooth, lacquered surface—all these things are important to instrument construction, and Randy was learning about them before he even knew how he would apply the knowledge. In time he would understand the luthier's fundamental challenge: coercing a tree to sing.

2

MERGING PATHWAYS

*There's got to be a better way to live than waiting for Friday
to come so you don't have to go to work the next day.*

———

RANDY WOOD

Ask Randy how he learned to tackle the challenges of lutherie, and his answer is likely to frustrate anyone looking for a shortcut to mastery. "I depend a lot on my eye and feel." A luthier must know the wood intimately, how easily it carves, how it splinters, and yes, how it feels. Randy developed this feel at an early age. And as he was developing the personality and skills that would lay the foundation for his career in music, the courses of country and bluegrass music were on trajectories that would eventually merge with Randy's in a big way. That intersection would take place in Nashville in the 1970s, but Nashville and the music industry seemed far away from the Wood household in which Randy was born.

Douglas, Georgia

Randy can thank music for his arrival into this world because it brought his parents together. His father, Bob Wood, played guitar and harmonica. He also sang in a gospel quartet with his brothers. "That's how I think he met Mama, playing at a square dance," Randy explains. Over a period of nearly two decades following that fateful square dance, Bob and Cora Wood raised six children. First among them was Joan, born in 1936. A sister, Jean, followed in 1939. On August 11, 1943, the first boys arrived as twins, born in a farmhouse in rural Georgia, between the towns of Broxton and Douglas. Bob Wood gave his name to each of the boys who shared the title of firstborn son. Bob's full name was John Robert Wood; the first twin was named John Reginald. The second was Robert Randall. Both boys would be known throughout their lives by their shortened middle names, Reggie and Randy. The two boys were followed by another sister, Joyce, and then nearly eleven years later by another brother, Bruce.

Randy Wood arrived in this world as World War II was raging across Europe and the Pacific. Many were compelled to work long hours and ration precious goods in support of the war effort. Randy knew about hard work and a meager existence firsthand, but for a different reason. His early childhood was spent on a farm as a sharecropper's son. Even though Randy's family did not own the land on which he was raised, Randy's roots run deep in the swampy southern Georgia farm country. He remembers his grandparents' nearby farm in what was once the town of Shepherd. The farm had a twenty-acre field with a well that once served as the town water supply before General Sherman wiped the town off the map during the Civil War.

From an early age, Randy worked the farm with his father and uncles. Chopping, sawing, and carving wood were all necessary farm tasks. "On a working farm, from the time you're born, you're working with wood. You're cuttin' stove wood or using a saw. Until I was six years old, we didn't even have electricity, so we heated with wood; we cooked with wood. We had to go out and cut all that wood, even at that early age. You just grow up around it, and you do it," Randy explains.

Randy remembers receiving a significant gift early in his childhood: his first pocket knife. The gift came with a lesson, too. "When I was five years old, I would borrow my dad's pocket knife. I loved to whittle. I lost that pocket knife one time and got one of the worst whippings that I think I ever got. But, also, the next month when Daddy and Mama went to town, he brought me back a pocket knife of my own. I never did lose that knife again." The same year that Randy received that knife, Bob Wood began work as a pine resin harvester for turpentine production. Randy studied his father at work, and he recalls,

In order to harvest that resin, you nail a small metal box to the base of a pine tree, and then you take a tool that cuts a groove, called a hack, and you cut a couple of grooves—just like the stripes on a sergeant's sleeve—in the side of that tree, just above the box. The pine tar runs out of that and into that cup. Then every week you go back to it and you make two more cuts above that and just keep cuttin'. Those things will sometimes get to be four or five feet long. They call those "cat faces."

Randy's eye for detail developed early, as is evident from his vivid memory of the harvesting process.

As a boy who watched his father closely, Randy relished praise from Bob Wood. His memory of one particular moment is testament to the impact such praise had on the impressionable child. When Randy was nine years old, the Wood family relocated to Douglas, Georgia, where Bob had an opportunity to take part ownership in a small dairy farm. One day Randy accompanied his father to town, where Bob promised to buy a balsa wood model airplane kit Randy had been longing to have. When they arrived at the hobby shop, Bob showed the store clerk the model kit Randy wanted. The clerk must have seen Randy and questioned whether he was old enough to build such a complex model. "I remember Daddy telling him, 'Well, he's had a pocket knife ever since he's been able to walk, just about. He can take a pocket knife and make anything he wants to.' That has always stuck with me."

It is unlikely Bob Wood could have predicted the impact that compliment had on his son. Randy has cared for rare instruments worth hundreds of thousands of dollars. He has relied on supreme confidence to dismantle these rare treasures and put them back together—confidence fostered by his father's approval. Recognizing the impact that well-placed praise can have, Randy has since tried to acknowledge talent when he sees it. "I've always tried to give people encouragement and praise people, especially kids," he says. "If a kid did a good job, I always tried to give them the recognition—not cover them up with praise—but at least give them the recognition that they did a good job in the hope that later on in life that might have some impact on them." Later in his career, Randy's apprentices would learn that praise did not flow so easily from him. But his judicious release of affirmation only amplified its impact when he offered it.

While building model airplanes entertained Randy in his free time, he had precious little of it to enjoy. Randy remembers having to wake up in the dark hours of the morning before school to help milk cows. And he was often called upon to help fix farm equipment. "Something was always getting broke around the farm," he told *Savannah Morning News* reporter J. R. Roseberry (1998).

Brunswick

In 1955, when Randy was eleven, his family moved again, this time to the coastal town of Brunswick, Georgia, where his father found work first as a carpenter and then in a boatyard. Through his example, Bob Wood sent the message that an opportunity for work should not be wasted, even if it required relocating a large family with young children.

Randy also got the message that he needed to work and develop employable skills while he was in school. Fortunately, Glynn Academy had a strong industrial arts program. His curriculum included two years each of wood shop, machine shop, and drafting classes. To a farm boy who grew up around tools, wood shop and machine shop classes were natural environments. But Randy was most drawn to drafting classes. "Drafting was something I could start making a living at right away. I'd rather sit in an office and draw than be out on top of a building putting a roof on. I always enjoyed drawing, so that seemed like the path of least resistance at the time. I figured I would become a draftsman, which is what I did." A draftsman relies on his steady hand and eye for detail, skills Randy had been honing since he started whittling at the age of five. His instructors recognized his ability and named him a junior instructor. To this day, Wood still considers himself a draftsman by trade (Roseberry 1998).

The independence and self-sufficiency that would be Randy's hallmarks as an adult began to surface while he was in high school. After his sophomore year, Randy spent the summer in New Smyrna Beach, Florida, with a friend whose father worked in a garage. There Randy earned money performing oil changes. "I had to lie to him and tell him that I was eighteen," he says. During the summer between his junior and senior years, Randy followed a friend to Winter Haven, Florida, to work. Remarkably, Randy's parents did not put up any resistance to his moving out for the summer, but they did not offer any financial support, either. "I had to fend for myself. They didn't give me no money or nothing. I went down there and got me a job. But getting out and doing stuff like that, you get used to doing stuff for yourself. You're not around your parents all the time."

Randy believes the self-sufficiency he displayed was shaped by his struggle for the rewards that appeared to come so easily to his twin brother, Reggie. "He was always the biggest, the most popular. I can hardly ever remember him bringing a book home from school, and he always made As and Bs. He never studied. If he saw a guitar, he could go over and pick a tune out. It all came easy to him. I worked my tail off for everything I got. I always had an arm full of books at home just trying to pass. I was always kinda walking in his shadow."

But in Reggie's shadow Randy discovered an important life lesson. Randy's struggles to match his twin brother instilled in Randy a sense of confidence in his ability to rationally work through a problem and arrive at a decision. "I made a decision early on, when you come up to a point where you have to make a decision about something, you try to study every angle, and then you make a decision based on that rather than a decision based on feeling. And then you go with it. You've made a choice. You've done something, and then you live by that decision. That's something I've always tried to do. I've always felt that by doing that, I could always look back and say I studied the situation and made the best decision at that time." This revelation gave Randy an air of wisdom that made him seem mature beyond his years. And it changed the arc of his life, as his decisions took him on a path that branched away from the path trod by his father and brother. "I've always felt that my dad and my brother would take the path of least resistance. As long as they didn't have to make any big decisions, they just kinda rolled with the flow. Both of them had opportunities far beyond what they utilized. Not that they didn't do all right, but I've felt like either of them could have done a lot better, because they certainly had the ability."

Country Music's Merging Path in the 1940s and 1950s

Long before Randy learned how to live by the merit of his own efforts, the city where he burnished his reputation took its first step toward becoming "Music City." And the personalities who would play significant roles in Randy's career were rising to prominence.

In 1925 the National Life and Accident Insurance Company, in search of a new way to market its services, launched its own radio station, WSM, in Nashville. WSM began broadcasting the *WSM Barn Dance,* which soon became the *Grand Ole Opry.*

The *Opry* brought country music and its personalities, such as Bill Monroe and Roy Acuff, to the masses. Monroe, with his mournful voice and powerful mandolin chop, enchanted listeners across the entire reach of WSM, which as a clear-channel station was vast. Acuff was one of country music's first big celebrities. His regular appearances on the weekly show "transformed the *Grand Ole Opry* from a barn dance to a national program for featuring star talent" (Malone 1968, 213). Acuff was also a savvy music businessman, securing the publishing rights to a huge catalog of songs through his company, Acuff-Rose. Randy Wood benefited in later years from Acuff's frequent visits to Wood's establishment. Acuff's association with him gave Randy instant credibility.

Bill Monroe's eventual fame worked in Randy's favor, too. Monroe made his name by the musical genre he fathered. He absorbed the sounds he heard from his childhood in Kentucky and created a groundbreaking style all his own, mixing blues, hillbilly, and old-time music. Monroe began performing with his brothers in 1927, but his recordings with his brother Charlie ignited his career. Between 1936 and 1938, Bill and Charlie recorded sixty songs about love and loss, sung in high, tight harmony. These tunes foreshadowed the style that would become bluegrass. The brothers disbanded, and Bill formed his own band, known as the Blue Grass Boys. Monroe fronted the band playing his iconic Gibson F-5 mandolin. In the 1970s Monroe entrusted his famous instrument to Randy for maintenance.

The Blue Grass Boys initially enjoyed regional success, but in 1945 a young banjo player named Earl Scruggs joined the band and helped it put bluegrass "on a national stage" (Malone 1968, 314). Scruggs played the banjo with a three-finger style producing rolling, syncopated notes intertwined with the melodies he picked. The sound captivated both live audiences and the broader radio audience of WSM's *Grand Ole Opry*. While Bill Monroe frequently reshuffled his lineup of Blue Grass Boys, the incarnation with Scruggs as well as guitarist and vocalist Lester Flatt was considered by many to be the groundbreaking bluegrass group.

The Blue Grass Boys broadened the nation's interest in acoustic instruments. Monroe's virtuosity inspired countless mandolin players. Thanks to Monroe, the Gibson F-5 mandolin he played became one of the requisite instruments in any band claiming to play bluegrass. Likewise, Lester Flatt set the standard for rhythm guitar playing in bluegrass bands, even popularizing a run of bass notes between verses that became known as the "Lester Flatt Run." And it is impossible to overstate Earl Scruggs's influence on the banjo. Before Scruggs arrived on the scene, the banjo in country music had not been regarded as a serious instrument worthy of mastery. It was more likely used as a comedic prop. But Scruggs's three-finger roll, executed with impeccable timing and intonation, raised the standard of musicianship that audiences could expect to be demonstrated on this hillbilly instrument.

Meanwhile, the postwar economic lift gave Americans newly disposable income for spending on hobbies. This triggered a buying spree of instruments from makers such as Gibson and Martin. Martin, for example, sold approximately 2,500 guitars in 1933. By the beginning of the 1960s, that number increased to more than 5,500 and grew to more than 14,000 by the end of 1969 (Longworth, Johnston, and Boak 2008). Unfortunately, the binge also had its letdown. Troves of lightly played instruments found their way into the back corners of closets and attics after the owners realized copying a sound like Scruggs's banjo style took years of diligent practice. Years later, a new wave of bluegrass fans began to value the vintage instruments that their heroes played. Their interest drove a demand to dig out the neglected instruments from their dark hiding places. But the instruments would need reviving. Randy Wood found himself poised to bring these old treasures back to life.

The postwar era saw the continued growth of country music and the unchallenged establishment of Nashville as its center. The *Opry*, recorded at the Ryman Auditorium in downtown Nashville, had become "king of the barn dances" (Malone 1968, 212), with its popularity even surpassing Chicago's *WLS Barn Dance*, on which the *Grand Ole Opry* was modeled. There were other popular barn dance radio programs, such as *The Louisiana Hayride*, broadcast from Shreveport, Louisiana. But the *Hayride* never retained the talent of the *Opry*. *The Louisiana Hayride* essentially became a minor league farm team for the major league stage at the Ryman, a stepping-stone for rising stars. Ever since Roy Acuff helped turn the *Opry* into a showcase for star talent, bands continued to mold the definition of country and bluegrass music. Of course, Bill Monroe was a perennial figure. In 1948 Flatt and Scruggs left Monroe and formed their own band, which was just as groundbreaking as Monroe's.

Country music was also incorporating provocative new sounds. Brothers Ralph and Carter Stanley brought the rustic tunes of the Appalachian Mountains to country music audiences. In the late 1940s, Merle Travis established a unique style with his virtuosic guitar-picking—on a guitar that Randy would eventually repair—and songs of the trials in the lives of coal miners. His music was reminiscent of western and honky-tonk. And in the late 1940s, the quintessential honky-tonk musician Hank Williams recorded "Lovesick Blues," a song whose popularity put him on the map of national consciousness.

Moving into the 1950s, country music experienced one of many identity crises that continue to this day. What exactly makes music "country"? In the more traditional country camp, the *Grand Ole Opry* grew, and many of the biggest names in country music were members. By 1950 the cast of the show had grown to about 120 (Malone 1968, 213). But with the increasing popularity of country music, more pop elements emerged. Electric instruments became widespread (Malone 1968, 228). The fiddle disappeared from country songs. Even Eddy Arnold, one of the biggest names in country music in the late 1940s, smoothed his style and image in the 1950s after having achieved success, shedding some of his "rustic simplicity and sincerity" of his days as a strictly hillbilly singer (Malone 1968, 224).

Regardless how the country genre was defined, Nashville solidified itself as the wellspring of successful music. In 1955 two brothers, Owen and Harold Bradley, boosted Nashville's reputation when they built a Quonset hut studio in the backyard of a house on what would become known as Music Row. A few blocks away, RCA Victor later built its own studio, overseen by guitarist Chet Atkins. Nashville became *the* place to record music. As studios sprouted, session musicians proliferated, feeding off the competition to raise the bar of performance. By the late 1950s "Nashville musicians were in the vanguard" of performers in any genre (Malone 1968, 253).

One effect of the incubation of talent in Nashville's studios was the development of the "Nashville sound," characterized by clean instrumental styles, usually electrified and devoid of the rustic elements of fiddle and banjo. Orchestral arrangements and smooth vocal harmonies were prevalent, too (Kosser 2006, 42). Some country music purists began to feel that the music was becoming too slick. Some of these disheartened country fans became loyal patrons to Randy Wood's nightclub in the Old Time Picking Parlor in the 1970s. There they found in Randy a music promoter who valued authentic talent and musicianship.

In 1954 Mississippi farm boy Elvis Presley signed a recording contract with Sun Records and launched the rock-and-roll boom. In 1956 Presley came to Nashville to record "Heartbreak Hotel" at Trafco Studio, not far from the Bradleys' studio (Kosser 2006, 15). The success of that record attracted rock-and-roll artists to Nashville in search of the next big hit. The mingling of the country and rock musicians further blurred the lines between the two genres.

Country music became lucrative, but many asked, "Is it still country?" (Malone 1968, 276). Some of the same people asking that question launched a traditional renaissance. "Developing in the midst of country music's growing sophistication and commercialization, therefore, and in large part in reaction against it, was a traditional renaissance," writes historian Bill Malone (1968, 279). Bluegrass music, in particular, flourished among people who still longed for the excitement of live shows, even despite—or because of—the occasional lack of polish inherent in live, improvisational music. No group saw as much success as Flatt and Scruggs (Malone 1968, 320). They joined the *Grand Ole Opry* in 1955 and toured extensively throughout the Southeast and then from coast to coast, enjoying the financial support of their nationally recognized sponsor, Martha White Flour. The band's popularity inspired a generation of banjoists, rhythm guitar players, fiddlers, and Dobro players. But success by bluegrass standards paled in comparison to the fame that Elvis and the purveyors of the Nashville Sound achieved.

America's consciousness of acoustic music expanded with the urban folk revival. City-dwellers who wanted something that was not exactly rock-and-roll or pop, more sophisticated than rural bluegrass, found it in such bands as the Kingston Trio. Their version of "Tom Dooley" was a hit in 1958 and spawned numerous vocal trios and quartets. The popularity of the Kingston Trio rekindled the nation's interest in the instruments that both urban folk and bluegrass musicians played.

While Nashville developed its reputation as Music City, country music alienated those responsible for its birth. As starry-eyed musicians flocked to the Tennessee capital to find their big break, some would say there was a gap emerging between the city-slicker performers and the people for whom honky-tonk and mountain music described familiar ways of life. There was a lack of authenticity. However, by the mid-1970s, Randy Wood had become a beacon of authenticity in his shop in downtown Nashville.

The Army Calls

The developments in Nashville must have seemed to Randy as though they were taking place in another world. By his senior year of high school in 1961, he faced a big step: what to do after graduation. With his aptitude for drafting, Wood considered becoming an engineer and was given assurance by an army recruiter that he would be able to attend engineering school if he joined the military. That was enough to convince Randy, and he signed up in July 1961, just two weeks after graduating from Glynn Academy and just as the United States' presence in Vietnam was growing.

Boot camp, while grueling, instilled in Randy lessons he has carried for a lifetime. The teamwork necessary for survival in basic training taught him acceptance, a skill that would serve him well later when he would open his doors to all types of people that the music world would throw at him. "Boot camp was kind of like a rite of passage," he explains. "You meet people from everything imaginable in there, and you gotta get along. Ain't no ifs, ands, or buts about it. You're on your own. You're responsible for yourself. You ain't got Mama and Daddy," he says, echoing the lesson he learned while living away from home during summers in high school. But Randy was not intimidated. "I look at it as a new experience. Look forward to it. That's the way I've always done stuff like that. I always look forward to a new adventure."

When he enlisted at Fort Jackson near Columbia, South Carolina, he was told that the engineering school was full, and he would have to wait eight months for a slot to open. For someone accustomed to hard work, the prospect of biding time had little appeal. Instead, Randy accepted an offer to go immediately into the Army Security Agency (ASA). From September 1961 through the spring of 1962, he trained at Fort Devens, near Boston. "That place was a mess, right in the middle of the snow belt." Cold weather may have seemed like the worst threat in the ASA, but he soon learned otherwise. "Four guys that I went to ASA school with at Fort Devens got killed. Those guys had gotten out six weeks ahead of me— they were in the next class in front of me—and they went straight to Thailand and were killed when someone threw a hand grenade in a truck where they were." Randy's assignment turned out to be a more hospitable one in Hawaii, where his primary duty was monitoring communications from military installations in the Pacific. "I was in a little ol' place out in the middle of a pineapple patch called Aliamanu Radio Station. It was the second or third smallest army post in the world. In ASA, we only had sixty-five people, including officers, on post."

Randy's assignments required him to work between two locations in Hawaii: bustling Oahu and the quieter Big Island base camp. "There was nothing over there," Randy says of the Big Island. "We were out in the middle of nowhere and fifty miles from anything."

But the idle time provided something useful—the time to learn a new hobby. "That's basically where I sat down to teach myself guitar chords,"

Randy recalls. His guitar-playing progress was unremarkable until an automobile accident left him with a long recovery time that he filled with guitar practice. "I rolled a Jeep down the side of a mountain over there and busted up one of my legs," he explains with characteristic nonchalance. He spent two weeks in convalescent care, and then, since he was single and unable to work active duty, he was assigned to work in the hospital for about ten weeks while he continued his recovery. "I met this guy there who was a pretty good picker, and he started showing me how to use chords. We'd meet up in the day room, check out a couple of guitars, and sit there and play, playing mostly country music."

Randy enjoyed playing music, but he was particularly drawn to the instruments that were making it. After he recovered from his Jeep accident, Randy and his new friend spent their free time in music clubs in Honolulu. "There was a little club that had folk music, and there was a submarine guy from Texas, and he played the autoharp like Maybelle Carter. I mean, he could play the hell out of it. So we decided we needed us an autoharp." Randy and his buddy pooled their money and bought one. "Of course, he could hardly play the radio, so I wound up with the autoharp."

Despite his army post's small size, it had a well-stocked wood shop that Randy visited frequently. He felt at home working with wood again and soon found opportunities for side jobs there. "We had a better wood shop than Schofield Barracks did, and Schofield Barracks had 20,000 people," Randy claims. "When I got there, there was a sergeant who was in charge of it, and I started going down there all the time, piddling around. When the sergeant got transferred, they didn't have anybody to run it, so they turned it over to me. So I started spending most of my time there."

In 1964, after three years of military service, Randy left the army and returned to Brunswick to resume civilian life. He converted a tool shed behind his parents' house into "a little efficiency apartment." When he was not working, he was eager to find outlets for his new hobby of playing music. He and his brother, along with three others, formed a rock-and-roll band called the Swampmen. Randy and Reggie shared duties playing rhythm guitar and singing lead vocals. Rounding out the Swampmen were a bass player, drummer, and lead guitar player.

Randy's latent enterprising spirits surfaced when the band struggled to find dependable gigs. A nightclub called the Beachcomber, on nearby St. Simons Island, became available for rent, and Randy and two other friends decided they would try to run the club. He recalls:

> It was two blocks from the King & Prince Hotel, and it was the only rock-and-roll club that was in Glynn County. All the other rock-and-roll type clubs were in the city limits. The blue laws, being what they were back then—this being the middle of the Bible Belt—made all the clubs close at midnight in the city. But since we were in the county, we could stay open until 2 a.m., so we had a big advantage. Plus, we had, even if I do say so, a good rock-n-roll band.

Settling into a career was still far from his mind "When you're twenty-one," he says, "you're not thinking about making a living. You're just looking to have a good time."

Indeed, they were having a good time and even eking out a living. "One of the guys that was in the band, his family owned a little grocery store, so he had the money," Randy notes. The other partner in the club was in the military and stationed at nearby Glynco Naval Air Station. "Our thinking was if we had a nightclub that young women came to frequent, and we had a good rock-and-roll band, and if he'd spread the word around about it out at Glynco, then we would get all the navy guys coming over there, and we'd have a crowd of spending patrons." The memory reflects one of Randy's recurring dreams: to be the proprietor of a favorite hangout spot. Ultimately, the club did not depend solely on navy bachelors for business. "We had all the locals. On Friday night and especially Saturday night, you couldn't even get in the place. The parking lot would be full of people." For three nights a week, the Swampmen entertained the Brunswick crowds as the Beachcomber's house band.

One of those in the crowd one night was a tall, attractive young blonde named Irene. Having moved south from her home state of Ohio, "she was living in Brunswick, managing a dollar store down there." Irene became a frequent visitor to the club. She would have been hard to miss when she was in attendance. She flashed a megawatt smile, and as Doug Green would write in 1976, she had "the loveliest eyes in town." She was also outspoken and never afraid to express her honest opinions with friends

25

or strangers. Irene and Randy met between sets of a Swampmen performance, and they quickly hit it off. Her saucy candor intrigued the quiet Wood.

While operating the club, Wood also met Curtis Burch Jr., who would later play Dobro in the groundbreaking New Grass Revival. Their friendship proved to be influential for Randy, as it was one of the first that began to bend the arc of his life toward bluegrass. Burch's father worked for the local beer distributor who supplied the Beachcomber. The senior Burch told Randy that he and his sons played in a bluegrass group. He asked if they could play at the club sometime. "I told him, yeah. We couldn't do anything at night, but on Saturday afternoons we could open up and do bluegrass until six o'clock or so. So we started doing that, and I started playing with them."

Playing in the house band brought with it the responsibility of maintaining instruments. Being a natural tinkerer, Randy made repairs to his own instruments, and his bandmates noticed his mechanical aptitude. "Other people in the band started asking me to work on their instruments and their friends would come to me," he recounted in an interview with J. R. Roseberry for the *Savannah Morning News*. As Randy tinkered with instruments, he began thinking about building his own. "After I started foolin' with 'em, I kind of always wanted to build one," he told Roseberry (1998).

Running a club and playing music were what Randy wanted to do. He enjoyed his life, but it soon became apparent to Randy that most people were not so fortunate. Randy's life at that point, while not extravagant, was at least interesting. The civilian working world was still new to him, though. Many of his contemporaries were more deeply entrenched in their jobs and domestic routines. Randy did not like what he saw.

When I got out of the service and went back home, I went over and stayed with my brother for a couple of weeks, just getting back into civilian life. I noticed that all the guys that we had gone to school with that didn't go into the service and stayed around, they had all gotten jobs and were working at factories and most of them married and had a kid or two. But, right off the bat, I noticed that the only thing they could talk about was looking forward to the weekend. They couldn't wait until Friday got there so they didn't have to get up the next morning and go to work, and 'oh how bad the job was,' and how bad they hated it. That was all everybody talked about. They couldn't wait until Friday because then they got a couple of days off. And I started thinking to myself, these guys are in a rut, and there's got to be a better way to live than waiting for Friday to come so you don't have to go to work the next day. That's got to be ridiculous to have to worry about getting up the next morning to go to work.

By his early twenties, Randy confronted a fear that would be present at most of his major career decisions. He feared becoming miserable through complacency. The prospect of not finding enjoyment in his daily work was so distasteful to him that he vowed to avoid falling victim to it. This vow to keep his life interesting was a turning point for Randy.

The Swampmen landed more gigs as their popularity grew, but their success peaked just shy of the critical mass necessary to make the band a viable career option for the members. "We started getting some offers to do some bigger things," Randy says. They received what seemed like the opportunity of a lifetime—a chance to play on the *Louisiana Hayride*. The offer came from a visitor to the Beachcomber who told Randy that he booked music for clubs around Louisiana and Texas and also for spots on the *Louisiana Hayride*. The offer excited Randy. "It was a big thing at that time. That was where Elvis got his start, Faron Young, Conway Twitty—lots of folks." But the response from the rest of the band was less enthusiastic. "Nobody could go but me. They were interested, but they couldn't afford to quit their day jobs. It just didn't work out." That offer to go on the *Hayride* gave Randy a whiff of bigger opportunities beyond Brunswick, and he grew restless with his status quo. "So I told them I'm not going to stay here and play at this club the rest of my life." Randy left the band and the club, explaining that he "just finally got burned out on music and nightlife and the whole nine yards."

3

THE MEANDERING ROAD
TOWARD NASHVILLE

If Tut had been building cabinets,
I'd probably be a cabinetmaker today.

———

RANDY WOOD

When Randy left the club and the band, he also parted ways with his source of income. What followed were a series of jobs that, while paying the bills, hardly provided fulfillment. Ever the pragmatist, Randy wasted no time changing course by putting down the guitar and picking up his drafting pens. He called a friend who worked as a surveyor for Glynn County who had been pestering Randy to come work for him drawing plats. When Randy called, the drafting job had been filled, but a survey crew had an opening. The job would be Randy's if he wanted it. Randy had no idea how grueling the work would be. "I didn't have no better sense than to do that," he says with a laugh. On his first day of work, Randy drove to Thalmann, fifteen miles outside of Brunswick, and learned the crew needed to survey a spur track to Cumberland Island, which "was about twenty-eight miles—and every bit of it just about through swamp. I spent that day cutting survey line with a bush hook. That was probably the worst day of my life. Well, maybe the next day was the worst day. The next morning I got up and didn't think I'd be able to move, I was so sore." The club life had taken its toll on Randy's fitness. "After a week of clearing survey lines, I started getting back into shape, because I had been way out of shape, living in clubs for damned near a year, playing, and raising hell." Rarely one to complain, Randy accepted the challenges of the new job.

He kept his eyes open for something more interesting, though, and he applied his work ethic to vie for a better position. After two weeks on the job, he noticed, "The guy running the transit is the best job to have if you're doing survey work." He was inspired: "I started learning everything there was to learn about a transit. About three weeks into it, he just turned the crew over to me, and from then on, I ran the levels and let somebody else cut the line."

Atlanta and Walter Butler's Jams

Survey work provided a living for almost a year, but Randy missed being around music. Along with his friend Curtis Burch Jr., he looked for outlets for their musical cravings. The two made connections in the thriving communities of bluegrass enthusiasts throughout Georgia. One of those connections proved to be catalytic in Randy's life. Walter Butler hosted weekend jams at his house near Atlanta, and Burch and Randy drove up to them regularly. Randy described Butler as "just a blue-collar worker, but he loved bluegrass music, and every six or eight weeks, he would have a pickin' at his house. He lived in a little old subdivision called Pine Lake, out near Stone Mountain. He was not a great singer or great player. He just loved bluegrass music as much as anybody you could ever imagine."

When quitting time arrived on Fridays, Randy and Burch set their sights northward toward Butler's jam, as many pickers did from across the region. Randy explains the weekly routine:

> When we would get off from work on Friday afternoon, we would meet at the Forks, just north of Brunswick, and I'd pick him up and we'd head for Atlanta on them old two-lane highways. It'd be one or two o'clock in the morning when we'd get there, but they'd be going full bore at Walter's. We'd jump out of the car and get in there and go with them. There was just some great pickin' going on. If you were

involved with bluegrass, you would probably hear about it. Butler's pickin' parties were historic. There'd be 150 people there, and this is out in the middle of an old subdivision.

Not all the neighbors were so enamored of the cacophony. "They raised all kinds of hell," Randy says. "Usually by sundown Friday afternoon, they'd have already called the cops." But in north Georgia, the police were likely to be bluegrass fans, too. "The cops usually would come out and just open the door to the car so they could hear the radio if they got a call, and they'd stand outside the car and listen to music. As a matter of fact, two or three of them played. One of them was a good banjo player," Randy claimed. (McDonald 1989).

Butler's frequent jams appealed to Randy, and he wanted closer access to Pine Lake. By mid-1966 he was also starting to feel the urge to make a change. The dreaded monotony had crept into his work life. An Atlanta-based engineering company approached Randy with an offer for a drafting job, and he accepted, recognizing that such a move would take him closer to Walter Butler. He promptly found an apartment a few blocks away from Pine Lake.

But there was one person Randy could not leave behind in Brunswick: Irene. What began as occasional weekend visits at the Beachcomber became a romantic relationship that Randy cherished. In June 1965 they decided to marry. They share a strong tendency toward pragmatism, and their wedding was a prime example. They drove down to Kingsland, Georgia, near the Florida-Georgia border. Randy says, "It's one of those marriage mill towns where you can go down there, and within an hour you can be married," which is what they did. With a job waiting and Walter Butler's jams calling for Randy, he and Irene wasted no time relocating. After their wedding, "I think we took off for Atlanta the next day," he claims.

Randy was happy with his new life. Describing his new routine, he says, "I would usually get home before Walter did, but I'd go on down there, and there would be three or four of us down there by five o'clock. We'd start picking then, and then the music didn't stop until Sunday afternoon." It is a testament to Irene's devotion that she tolerated her new husband's regular weekend forays away from home.

Enter Tut Taylor

Among the many pilgrims who flocked to Walter Butler's jams was Robert Taylor, a Dobro player from the central Georgia town of Milledgeville. Everyone knew him as "Tut." Tut was tall with a round build and thinning hair, giving him the look of the wise elder statesman of the crowd at Butler's parties. He spoke with the vocal rise and fall of an auctioneer in quick bursts, yet still maintaining the long vowels and the dropped r's of a southern dialect. He loved being the maestro of any gathering. Among musicians, Tut was recognizable for his unorthodox style of playing the Dobro guitar with a flat pick instead of the more typical style of playing with finger picks. Tut enjoyed defying convention.

Despite being twenty years older than Randy, Tut fell under the same spell of Butler's jams that captivated Randy and Burch. He also established himself as a regular at Butler's jams. Taylor remembers, "It was a hundred miles to Atlanta from where we lived, and a lot of weekends, man, we'd go up there Friday night and pick almost straight through until Sunday morning and then come back home." Tut also enjoyed another arm of the bluegrass experience: instrument collecting. Tut relished old-fashioned deal-making. Through instrument trading and collecting, he could combine his knack for negotiating with his interest in music. Tut was an avid collector and had developed a reputation as a shrewd horse trader. Butler's jams represented a focused market for his trading hobby.

Tut longed for his own community of musicians in his hometown of Milledgeville. Randy recalls, "Every time Tut would come up there, he would be after me and Curtis Jr. to move to Milledgeville, because he needed somebody down there to play with." Taylor complained often to Randy and Curtis about the lack of pickers in his hometown. "That was what we heard every time we ran into him."

In September 1966, not long after the Woods moved to Atlanta, Irene gave birth to their first and only child, Renee. For many, a first child signals a new chapter in an adult life in which stability takes on more value than it did in carefree days of youth. Not for Randy. The prospect of boredom was far more worrisome than the hassle of relocating.

Moving to Milledgeville

Tut Taylor must have sensed Randy's wanderlust. Years of deal making had sharpened his eye for what makes people tick. Tut could be very persuasive when he wanted to be. After nearly a year of getting ambivalent responses to his suggestions that Randy and Curtis should move to Milledgeville, Tut tried a different tactic, and this time it worked. "Finally after over a year," Randy says, "he mentioned something about having a wood shop down there." That got Randy's attention, as he did not have access to a shop at the time. When he found out Taylor had a wood shop, Randy began negotiating, telling him, "If I can hang out in the wood shop when I'm not working, if you'll find me a good job down there, I'll move down there." Taylor held up his end of the bargain. "Hell," Randy exclaims, "about a couple weeks later he called and said, 'I've got you a job.' So I had to go ahead and move then." At the age of twenty-three, Randy once again uprooted his family, which now included a six-month-old daughter, and moved south to Milledgeville (DeYoung 2009).

Tut's shop is where Randy began to learn about instrument repair. To this day, Randy readily acknowledges he entered the field of lutherie because Tut was repairing instruments. Randy recounted in an interview with Pat Ahrens, "If [Tut] had been building cabinets, I'd probably be a cabinetmaker today" (P. J. Ahrens 2004). Instead, Tut "piddled around with instruments, mostly Dobros and banjos and mandolins."

Randy enjoyed having unrestricted access to Taylor's wood shop, but finding satisfaction at work was a different matter. Randy took the drafting job at a local pipe manufacturer Tut had found for him, but he quickly realized he was in over his head. "They hired me as a draftsman, but the engineer had retired, and so they wanted me to start doing his work, and I was by no means an engineer, especially doing some of the stuff they wanted done." The company was developing high-pressure hydraulic equipment that pushed the limits of conventional components. It was not work for an untrained engineer. "I would call some company to get hose that would withstand three million psi," Randy recalls, "and the people would laugh and hang up the phone." Randy soon realized it was a dead-end job. He stayed in it only one year. "I enjoyed it and learned a lot," he says in retrospect, "but they finally realized that they were going to have to get an engineer." Randy did not sit idle for long, though. He soon found a drafting job in the engineering department of the state hospital in Milledgeville. "You couldn't make any money in that," he claims. However, the main motivator in his life then was not money; it was woodworking. Describing his routine, Randy says, "I was going over to Tut's every night, working on instruments, working in the wood shop. I hated getting up in the morning and going to work, but I looked forward to getting off that evening and going to Tut's." He summarizes how he divided his attention: "If I wasn't working, I was over at Tut's, pretty much day and night."

Randy's youthful energy inspired Tut, and the two fed off each other's passion for working in the wood shop, developing their craftsmanship concurrently. "Randy was a good craftsman and a good learner," Taylor says. "Of course, I was learning, too, at that time. Back in that particular time period, information on instruments was very scarce. You didn't have a lot to look at or go by, or check out, or anything. So we got interested, needless to say. We were trying to glean information from every source." As an example, Taylor remembers struggling to learn how to fill in the tiny spaces in mother-of-pearl inlays on headstocks and fingerboards. He consulted a friend and fellow luthier. Naturally, he coaxed a solution out of him by making a deal. "He knew what the filler was," Taylor says, "and I forgot what I promised him if he would tell me—it was something. He told me, and all it was was epoxy with a little black color and some ebony dust. That's all there was to it. But like anything else, if you don't know, you could never guess."

In retrospect, it is clear Tut had something more valuable for Randy than free access to a wood shop. Tut had connections. In the late 1960s, even those performers who were country music royalty were not out of reach of a rural Georgia music fan such as Taylor. Tut had friends active in the country and bluegrass scene, and many stopped to visit if they were traveling through the area. Roy Acuff, the "King of Country Music," once paid a visit to Tut to discuss a possible deal to buy a collection of Dobros Tut owned. The deal never materialized, but because of the visit, Randy befriended Acuff and "Bashful Brother Oswald" Kirby, the Dobro player in Acuff's band. Randy also met such talents as fiddler Vassar Clements, Jake Landers, Herschel Sizemore, and banjoist and onetime Blue Grass Boy Rual Yarbrough. That group of musicians once spent an evening at Tut's while rehearsing for an album. "They came over New Year's Day of 1967 to rehearse doing that album," Randy recounts, "and it wound up being just an all-day, all-night jam session, which I loved. It was great, especially playing with people of that caliber."

Bob Givens

Of all the people Randy met at Tut's, none inspired him quite like Bob Givens. While Givens helped Randy hone his lutherie ability, he also tested the open-mindedness Randy had learned in boot camp. Indeed, Givens was practically Wood's polar opposite. He was a West Coast native and a draft dodger; Wood had recently completed service in the army. Givens bathed only occasionally; Wood sported neatly combed hair and side-burns and wore pressed, buttoned shirts with the front pocket brimming with pens, scales, and mini screwdrivers. Yet Givens was a luthier and top-notch craftsman, and for Randy, that was the only credential that mattered. "The big thing was Bob Givens coming around," Randy says of the influence Givens had on him. "That was probably one of the biggest turning points, because Bob had been doing instrument repair work and building, especially banjo necks."

Bob Givens was from California and had met Tut during one of Tut's an-nual trips to the West Coast. When the threat of the draft emerged, Givens and a friend drove to South America. "They were going to build a boat down there and start bringing Honduras mahogany to the States and sell-ing it," Randy claims. "Well, they got started building their boat, but they never did get it built, as far as I know. For one reason or another they ran out of money. They couldn't go back to California because the draft board was looking for them. So they decided to come to Tut's." Tut welcomed them with open arms. Randy continues, "They had a Land Rover, and they drove that thing all the way from Central America, all the way across the Panama Canal, all the way up through Mexico, to Tut's—nonstop. When they got to Tut's, they didn't have a dime. They didn't have any gas in that Land Rover. It just looked like a red ball of mud. And they did, too! It was the damnedest sight you ever saw in your life for them to come rolling into Tut's yard in that thing."

Bob Givens was gutsier about experimentation in Tut's shop than Randy. But Randy was a quick study. He observed Givens employ no-nonsense techniques to solve problems that had vexed Randy. "Bob was a hell of a craftsman, and I learned a lot from Bob," Randy admits. "A lot of stuff we figured out together, but a lot of the stuff I was doing at the time or trying to figure out, Bob had already done. One of them was cutting pearl." Randy had struggled for months to make progress using his pocket knife to cut pearl for inlays. "Bob showed me what a jeweler's saw was."

Givens was also a model of fanatical intensity on a project. Randy had begun building a mandolin and was only half-finished when Givens showed up at Tut's. "Bob had been there about a week," Randy says, "and he started looking at the mandolin and thought that'd be real interesting to build a mandolin, so he started building one." Despite Randy's head start, Givens and he finished their mandolins at the same time, thanks to Givens's manic pace. "He would work three or four days, twenty-four hours a day, and then he would crash for two or three days," Randy says incredulously. "And he would basically live on Dr. Peppers. It beat anything I had ever seen. Tut would go buy Dr. Peppers by the case and bring them in there." Randy mainly avoided Givens's mania, but Givens remained inspirational. "I began learning from Tut and Bob Givens and more or less picked up the rest on my own," Wood later told *Pickin'* (Buckingham 1976).

Tut Taylor was a sign painter by trade, but he repaired his friends' instruments in his shop in his spare time. Randy assisted when he saw repair projects matching his skill level. Common tasks included gluing cracks in the body of a guitar, replacing worn frets, and resetting guitar necks to correct the action height. Through that work, Randy saw repairing instruments as a way of making additional money, in addition to being an enjoyable avocation.

Country Music in the 1960s

As Randy inched closer to Nashville via Brunswick, Atlanta, and Milledgeville in the mid-1960s, country music continued to grapple with its identity. The doors were opening to more performers, and television proved itself as a new medium capable of reaching out to an ever broader audience. Randy may not have recognized it at the time, but the popularization of country music veered the genre away from its rustic, rural, authentic foundation. It was a music style that had grown up and left home. Randy would help bring a sense of authenticity back to Nashville.

Despite country music's evolution, Nashville maintained its position as the Music City. The "Nashville sound" grew even more refined, personified by the talents of Chet Atkins, Floyd Cramer, Buddy Harman, Bob Moore, Grady Martin, and Hank Garland, who contributed their talents to countless recording sessions taking place on Music Row. Other musicians (and music publishing companies) wanted a piece of the action. Recording studios stayed booked. The Bradley Studios and RCA Victor studios were two of the busiest. By the early 1960s, the Bradley Studios recorded about seven hundred sessions per year (Malone 1968, 262). The Nashville sound blurred the lines between pop and country and made country more appealing to a large audience. Country music's commercial viability throughout the 1960s produced names that still define the genre today. Singers and songwriters such as Willie Nelson, Hank Cochran, Harlan Howard, and Kris Kristofferson enjoyed great popularity and boosted the economic gains of the country music industry and, by association, Nashville.

Also, country audiences in the 1960s showed the industry that men were not the only ones who could generate big sales in the genre. Patsy Cline had a huge hit in 1960 with "I Fall to Pieces," and Loretta Lynn emerged on the scene in 1962 with her first big song, "Success" (Malone 2010). Dolly Parton arrived in Nashville in 1964 and would use her role as a performer on Porter Wagoner's television show to catapult her own career. Tammy Wynette became a household name with hits such as "D-I-V-O-R-C-E" and "Stand by Your Man."

Some fans, however, still longed for music that was closer to country's honky-tonk roots. One way to find it was to look outside Nashville. Several musicians from California, including Wynn Stewart, Merle Haggard, and Buck Owens, gave identity to a subgenre that became known as the California sound or Bakersfield sound (Haggard was from Bakersfield). It was music that harkened back to older country styles and included fast tempos and high-pitched steel guitar riffs (Malone 1968, 291). The image of the Bakersfield sound was also edgier than the styles coming out of Nashville. Haggard's gritty brand, in particular, benefited from his reputation for having served some prison time (Malone 2010).

George Jones and Waylon Jennings also nudged the center of gravity of country music slightly west of Nashville. While he gained popularity coming up through the ranks of the *Louisiana Hayride* and the *Grand Ole Opry*, Jones's Texas roots were a strong part of his identity as he dominated the charts in the 1960s with such hits as "Tender Years" and "She Thinks I Still Care." Jennings, another Texan, personified the "Outlaw" movement in country music, along with Willie Nelson and the Glaser Brothers. Their antiestablishment image, while perhaps only existing in the marketing of label promoters, found a following among country music fans fed up with the perceived softening of the genre.

Folk and bluegrass continued to provide their own avenues for disheartened country fans. Bill Malone offers one explanation to the growing interest in roots and acoustic music. He explains it as

> a reaction against the noise and inanities of rock-and-roll and Tin Pan Alley popular music, and as a corresponding effort to find a simpler and more digestible musical expression. A highly complex and industrialized urban society, restless and ever changing, and beset by anxieties and nuclear fears, yearned to attach itself to something substantial and concrete. The folk movement, therefore, is partially an effort to find "roots" and regain the lost values of an earlier rural age. (Malone 1968, 336)

There were plenty of sources of anxiety, as the nightly news relayed scenes of civil rights riots, war carnage in Vietnam, and disheartening advances in Russia's space program.

The urban folk revival and bluegrass revival brought attention to artists who had been unknown beyond the South. Banjoists Dock Boggs and

Clarence Ashley and guitarist Doc Watson gained respect among young audiences. The Country Gentlemen, consisting of Charlie Waller, John Duffey, Eddie Adcock, and Tom Gray, found widespread support throughout the 1960s among classic and progressive bluegrass fans.

The revivals found a particularly strong following on college campuses. Young, educated people, who thought of bluegrass as "backwards" just a few years earlier, suddenly fell in love with bluegrass and bought banjos to try to emulate the sounds of Earl Scruggs's syncopated banjo playing (Malone 1968, 323). Malone observed an "enormous increase in the sale of banjos and guitars" in the late 1960s. This demand would fuel the vintage industry Randy helped to nurture.

The college crowd, without the responsibilities of careers and families, was free to travel during the summers, attending the growing circuit of bluegrass and folk music festivals that emerged. The first bluegrass festival was held in Luray, Virginia, in 1961. But the festival movement really gained steam when Carlton Haney promoted a festival in Roanoke, Virginia, in 1965. Large festivals proliferated throughout Virginia, North Carolina, Georgia, Tennessee, Indiana, and Texas. Downtown Nashville, Randy Wood's eventual working home, saw its share of college students, thanks to the proximity of colleges and universities including Vanderbilt, Belmont, and Lipscomb (Malone 2010).

This college audience was a generation with exposure to television and movies in their formative years. In 1962, the *Beverly Hillbillies* debuted and enjoyed wide popularity. Flatt and Scruggs recorded the show's opening song, "The Ballad of Jed Clampett," which showcased Scruggs's distinctive rolling banjo style, attracting a new wave of disciples to the banjo, the virtuoso Béla Fleck among them. Scruggs's work could also be heard by movie audiences. The Flatt and Scruggs tune "Foggy Mountain Breakdown" became commonly known as the *Bonnie and Clyde* theme song due to its prominence in the movie's soundtrack.

Four television shows were particularly influential in spreading country music's reach in America: Porter Wagoner's show, launched in 1960; *Glen Campbell's Goodtime Hour*, hosted by the popular singer/guitarist; *Hee Haw*, with its blend of musical performance and rural comedy; and the *Johnny Cash Show*. The *Cash* show would prove particularly instrumental in Randy Wood's career. From 1969 through 1971, Cash hosted the show at the Ryman Auditorium, featuring some of the top performers in country, folk, and rock-and-roll. Had there been no *Cash* show, Randy Wood might never have moved to Nashville. But Randy made one more turn on his meandering path before he set course for Nashville.

Muscle Shoals, Alabama

After spending little more than a year in Milledgeville, Randy's restlessness resurfaced. Just as Tut convinced Randy to move down to Milledgeville, their mutual friend Rual Yarbrough, the banjoist, lured Randy to another change of scenery. Yarbrough had a small instrument repair shop in Muscle Shoals, and he invited Randy to move to Alabama to work in the shop. "He told me that if I would move over there, he would build a bigger shop," Randy says. "So that sounded fine to me." Yarbrough even promised to find Randy a drafting job so he would have a dependable income. Offering access to a wood shop was a recruiting tactic similar to the one Tut employed, and it was equally effective.

Muscle Shoals in the late 1960s was an exciting place to be for someone interested in music. The city was beginning to hit its stride as the "Hit Recording Capital of the World," thanks to recordings such as "Steal Away" by Jimmy Hughes and "When a Man Loves a Woman" by Percy Sledge at area studios. Legendary producer Rick Hall's FAME Studios and the Muscle Shoals Sound Studio attracted a diverse set of musicians to northwest Alabama. Wilson Pickett, the Rolling Stones, Aretha Franklin, and Duane Allmann are just a few of the many who would record songs in Muscle Shoals. Rick Hall's in-house rhythm section, known as the Muscle Shoals sound and the "Swampers," left FAME to open their own studio across town. They, too, struck gold recording hits such as "Wild Horses" and "Brown Sugar" by the Rolling Stones and songs by Cher and Boz Scaggs. Notably, these studios were color-blind in their efforts to promote both white and black artists. The Muscle Shoals music scene was a safe haven in a state that had a volatile mix of racial tensions (Fuqua 2014). All of this activity gave the region a buzz that must have appealed to Randy. He had to feel some connection to a place becoming famous for the music produced by a group called the "Swampers," since he had once been in a band called the "Swampmen" himself.

Randy visited Muscle Shoals and liked both the area and the arrangement that Yarbrough offered. At Tut's, whenever Randy repaired instruments, Tut kept any money received from the instrument owner. "That was kind of our deal," Randy admits, recognizing his novice status in Milledgeville. "I was learning something, so I was willing to let him make the money as long as I had access to the shop and was learning things. Kind of like going to school, I guess." In contrast, Yarbrough offered Randy an even split of the proceeds. That sounded ideal to Randy. "So I moved over there and drew up a set of plans for a new music store with a shop in the back. Within probably two weeks of our moving over there, he had started breaking ground on a new building. So I thought that was great."

Leaving a job, moving to another city, and taking up new work had become normal behavior. However, his coworkers at stable government jobs at the Milledgeville state hospital thought otherwise. "When I told the people I was working with that I was going to quit this nice, cushy state job and go to work working on musical instruments, they thought that I had spent too much time at the mental hospital, and they were half-serious about committing me!" Randy exclaims. "They couldn't believe it. They'd just shake their head and say, 'You're doing *what*?'" As Wood later recalled in an interview, "Quitting a government job to go work on guitars, well, that was one of the craziest things they'd ever heard of. To the average person it was, because nobody was doing anything like that back then" (Gamble 2001). Notably, Randy found support at home for his decision to leave a stable job to follow his passion.

Randy dismissed the discouragement of his coworkers at the state hospital, but he was not reckless. Randy knew he needed a real job to supplement the income from instrument repair work and support his young family, so he made a trip over to Muscle Shoals prior to his move to secure a job as a draftsman for a metal building company. "The job that I had lined up, I think it was going to be six weeks before the job was open." Rual offered to match Randy's current pay if he would move to Muscle Shoals immediately and help in the music store.

Even though Randy left Tut Taylor's tutelage, the two parted ways on good terms and stayed in touch. It was fortunate for Randy, since Tut would again play a significant role in his career in a few years' time.

Randy's move to Muscle Shoals in the spring of 1968 was well timed. Bluegrass festivals were proliferating, and Rual Yarbrough knew many of the banjo players who attended them. The combination of increased festival activity and a well-connected partner opened a market for instrument repair work for Randy. He and Rual drove to bluegrass festivals on weekends and pitched their services for banjo neck repairs. "I was building banjo necks at that time," Randy says, "and Rual played banjo and knew a lot of the pickers." He continues:

> Rual had just bought a brand-new Ford van—an extended Ford van— and the first thing we did was tear the back seat out of it and build a little cot on one side, so that we could have a place to sleep. There'd be some weekends we'd hit four festivals on the same weekend, so we were either out drumming up business, or we were driving the whole weekend. So one of us would drive and the other would sleep. We would go to a festival and we would come back with a van full of instruments to work on."

The work came in faster than either Randy or Yarbrough anticipated, and before Randy realized what had happened, he was a full-time instrument repairman. "By the time the drafting job came open that I was supposed to go to, I was like three or four months behind on repair work," Randy says. "I was making more money doing the repairs than the drafting job was going to pay me, so I just called them and told them that I wasn't going to be able to do it." It was a pivotal career decision that Randy has never regretted.

Randy and Yarbrough attracted paying customers for an activity most people did not realize was a business. Randy explained, "We were trying to build a repair business, which there was none back then. Most people didn't know you could get instruments repaired, and you couldn't in most places. We were one of the first repair shops." People were starting to realize that the old instruments were nicer than the new instruments you could buy, but they had problems, because they needed repair work, and they needed neck sets—stuff like that, and nobody did that." The festival circuit became their marketplace. "Rual and I had to create a demand for work in the mid-Sixties," he recounted to *Savannah Magazine*. "We'd load up and go walk around, talk to people we knew, introduce ourselves to musicians, and tell them if you've got anything [that] needs repairing, that's what we're doing. We'd collect instruments, bring them back to the shop, fix them, and when we got them fixed, deliver them to the next festival" (Gamble 2001). The close-knit community of festivalgoers was remarkable; Randy and Rual could actually rely on seeing their customers at another bluegrass festival in a matter of several weeks.

Word of Randy and Rual's repair business spread, and notables in the country music scene took note. "Twice a month, Hank Williams Jr. would drive down from Nashville to bring me instruments to repair," Randy says, "and I had met Shot Jackson [musician and designer and builder of Sho-Bud guitars], and he was telling everybody about the repair work. So word got around."

A local newspaper from Muscle Shoals reported one of Williams's visits to Rual's shop. The paper quoted Hank Jr. saying, "I bring all my work to Randy. He is the finest instrument man in the business" (Overall 1969). The photograph accompanying the article shows Williams and Yarbrough inspecting an instrument while Randy looks on with a skeptical gaze, clearly unfazed by the presence of a celebrity such as Williams. In a later interview, Randy recalled how gracious Williams was when he visited from Nashville. Williams's first order of business upon reaching Muscle Shoals was usually to treat anyone in the shop to lunch at a local barbecue joint. Randy remembered that Williams would bring in his guitars and shout, "Lock the door! We're going to eat!" (DeYoung 2009).

In a few short years, Randy Wood developed a reputation among many notable musicians as the preeminent instrument repairman. He owed much to his Georgia farm experience for providing an important foundation on which his reputation could grow. Of all the skills that a young farm boy picks up, perhaps the most valuable for Randy was the confidence to know that if something was broken, he could fix it. That confidence permeated his pursuits, especially his decisions to outrun the looming threat of an unhappy existence. Even in his early adulthood, Randy wasted little time fretting over major life decisions. When he needed to make a change, he made it. When his band in Brunswick, the Swampmen, reached a dead end, he changed careers. When he tired of driving to Atlanta for Walter Butler's jams, he moved closer. When Tut Taylor offered unrestricted access to a wood shop, he practically moved into the shop. And when he saw the chance to make a living as an instrument repairman, he went for it. Never mind that most people had no idea anyone could make a living, much less, support a family that way. Randy had the self-assuredness to give it a try.

Randy's reputation as a luthier was spreading through his growing repair activity. But he needed to demonstrate he could build from scratch if he wanted to be considered a great luthier. He soon built three mandolins that acted like megaphones, announcing to the world Randy Wood's arrival as a serious luthier, worthy of respect from a wide audience.

4

THREE MANDOLINS

It has a sound very much like Bill's old F-5,
and it has a bunch more response.

———

RED HENRY
speaking about Randy Wood Mandolin #1

I listen to recordings that I've done with it,
and it just spoke out so well.

———

ROLAND WHITE
speaking about Randy Wood Mandolin #2

It's got as good a projection as any
instrument I've ever known.

———

RED HENRY
speaking about Randy Wood Mandolin #3

Lloyd Loar's Gold Standard

In 1911 a trim twenty-five-year-old man from Illinois began working as
a performing musician for the Gibson Mandolin-Guitar Manufacturing
Company in Kalamazoo, Michigan. He boasted a solid educational foundation, having studied music at the Oberlin Conservatory, and he was
proficient on the mandolin, piano, violin, viola, and mandola. In his job

with Gibson, he traveled the country showcasing what the instruments could do in the hands of a capable performer. His name was Lloyd Loar.

Seven years later, near the end of World War I, Loar signed up to be a concert entertainer for U.S. soldiers in Europe. Almost as soon as he arrived, in November 1918, the war ended. His trip was not in vain, though. With time to spare in Europe, Loar spent several months in Paris studying at the National Conservatory of Music and National Institute of Radio Engineering.

Loar returned to Gibson as an acoustical design consultant, and it was then he made his most significant contributions to the legacy of Gibson mandolins. He used his knowledge of physics along with his appreciation of music to guide the Gibson luthiers in crafting instruments that would define a golden era for the company. Loar borrowed design elements from violins—graduated sound boards and backs, longitudinal tone bars, elevated fret boards, and f-holes—and incorporated them into Gibson mandolin designs (Siminoff n.d.).

His most important contribution was the extensive use of tap-tuning, the process of adjusting the size of sound chambers and structural components of the instrument to resonate together at a particular note (Siminoff n.d.). It is this quality—all components of the instrument working together to produce a pleasing tone—that makes Loar's instruments legendary. He signed the inside of his mandolins, and today Loar-signed Gibson mandolins are regarded as the Stradivariuses of the mandolin world, fetching well over $100,000 when they happen to emerge on the market. Mandolin virtuoso Chris Thile calls his 1924 Loar F-5 "The Bank of Chris" because he poured all his savings into the purchase in 2007 (Stone 2008).

In the 1940s Bill Monroe introduced American audiences to the enchanting sounds of a Loar instrument. With his commanding tone emanating from a 1923 Loar mandolin, Monroe inspired an entire generation of mandolin players who grew up hearing him on broadcasts of the *Grand Ole Opry*. Then, in the 1960s, these impressionable listeners flocked to the budding bluegrass festival circuit, where crowds spent hours jamming to the songs they heard on their radios and vinyl record players. Despite growing demand for acoustic instruments, the then-current production models of instruments did not compare with the prewar instruments. In particular, the tone of modern mandolins of that time paled next to the mandolins designed and signed by Lloyd Loar. Hand-carving gave way to automated production. Tap-tuning ceded to beefier construction. In the minds of the manufacturers, the threat of future warranty repair claims overshadowed a delicate instrument's superior tonal qualities. As bluegrass enthusiasts awakened to realize the value of these limited-quantity prewar instruments, the timing was right for somebody to address the shortage of desirable instruments. The timing also happened to be right for Randy Wood to build his first mandolin.

Randy Wood #1

Randy learned about Loar mandolins from Tut. As an avid collector, Tut had secured several Loars for his personal collection, and Randy was drawn to their aesthetics and display of craftsmanship. "I thought they were real neat looking," he says of Tut's Loars. Randy realizes he was at the right place at the right time to learn lutherie. "When I came on," he says, "there were a wealth of nice old instruments around that I could study. You didn't have to physically take them apart to study them." Knowing the importance of the thickness of the top and back pieces of a mandolin, Randy used a set of long calipers to reach in through the f-holes and measure at various points the thickness of the tops and backs of Tut's Loars. "I would sometimes sit there for an hour or two, just figuring out how a particular detail was done," he claims. "I was fortunate to have those things physically in my hand." Tut and Randy *did* take some of them apart. The top was damaged on one particular Loar, so Tut removed the top to repair it. Randy says, "I was able to get some pretty good measurements on that," since both the inside and outside of the top were exposed.

Randy wanted to build an instrument of his own, and he thought a mandolin might be a good first project. "We're talking '60s," Randy says, "and the mandolins that Gibson was building at that time were terrible and got even worse. I figured that if I could build one of those, I might be able to sell something like that because you can't go to the store and buy one, you know, a good one." Building a mandolin was an ambitious goal for a new luthier, since truly great mandolins required careful carving to achieve satisfactory tonal quality. "It was kind of naïve thinking, since mandolins are twice as hard to build as a guitar" (Roseberry 1998). But the challenges of the mandolin—the graduated top and back, the curly headstock, the sinuous curves and delicate points of the body, the graduated finish colors, the intricate inlay work—appealed to Randy. "A mandolin seemed to be more artistic than a guitar" (Roseberry 1998).

The construction of Randy Wood #1 began in 1966 at Tut's shop in Milledgeville. It was a good place for a beginning instrument builder, since Tut had some unusual resources. According to Red Henry, the eventual owner of Randy Wood #1, "Tut Taylor had been accumulating not only mandolins but wood. He had gone to the Gibson Company and bought some old wood they had put away for a long time because they didn't have use for it anymore. One of the slabs of wood was for a mandocello back. It was an extremely tight-grained piece of very old maple that Gibson had put away. Randy used that piece of wood for the back of Randy Wood #1. It's sort of a cousin to the old Gibson F-5 mandolins, you might say."

Characteristically, Randy found ways around the challenges he encountered. Graduating the top and back of a mandolin can be a painstaking process. Luthiers usually accomplish the task with exacting hand-carving, planing, and sanding. It requires a steady hand and a lot of patience, but Randy found another way around the problem. "I probably could have carved it," he says, "but that being the first one, I didn't really know how you went about doing something like that. But the thing that made the most sense to me was Tut had a side arm grinder in the shop, and boy, you could move a lot of wood with that thing in a hurry." So Randy selected a power tool for a job usually reserved for a carving knife. "I'd never do it nowadays, but it worked." He took the unfinished mandolin to Muscle Shoals and finally completed it in 1967.

Randy tried to build such an exact replica of a Gibson F-5 mandolin that he even copied the Gibson branding on the headstock. As a result, nothing on the mandolin outwardly identifies it as the work of Randy Wood. Today Randy's instruments bear his own logo, but when he built his first mandolin, he undertook a novel project by replicating a Gibson mandolin. There was no protocol for how to do it. As mandolinist Tony Williamson said, "It was common, accepted practice in the violin world when you reproduce a certain maker's instrument, to reproduce the label and put it inside it. And it wasn't really so much an effort to swindle somebody, because the vintage instrument market was not really a big deal. But when Randy copied that, his first mandolin was kinda based on Bill Monroe's mandolin, and when he copied it, he copied it right down to the labels." Darryl Wolfe, an expert on Loar mandolins and author of the *F5 Journal*, agrees with Williamson. "It's not acceptable in this day and age, but it was absolutely expected then. People didn't really feel like they were ripping off Gibson or anything like that. If you had a mandolin, it had to say 'Gibson' on it. That's just the way it was. Nobody was making a mandolin that looked like a Gibson at the time."

The responsiveness of Randy Wood #1, the impressive volume, and even its appearance matched the qualities of Loar mandolins that players in the late 1960s coveted. Little did Randy know that his mandolin would help launch an industry of small luthier shops attempting to harness that famous Loar tone with their own F-5 replicas. Red Henry once told the *Savannah Morning News*, "It has a sound very much like Bill's old F-5, and it has a bunch more response. It's two or three times as loud, which means I can play it in jam sessions. I can play it on stage and hear myself. I won't ever get buried by the banjo" (Roseberry 1998). He beams when he talks about the importance of that first mandolin of Randy's. "It was the one that broke open and established the field of making F-5 copies," he says. "Randy was the one that kicked that off with his #1 mandolin." In fact, there were other F-5 replicas in existence before Randy completed #1. Frank Wakefield played a replica built by Tom Morgan in 1963. In 1966 Bill Monroe could be seen playing an F-5 replica built by Seth Summerfield.

But Randy's stood out because he eventually put one of his mandolins in Monroe's hands. Monroe owned it for the rest of his life. By the time Randy finished #1, he and Rual Yarbrough were frequently attending bluegrass festivals, and Randy saw Bill Monroe in a small beer joint in Cincinnati one night, where they visited backstage between Monroe's sets. "I had that mandolin with me," Randy says, "and during one of the breaks, we were sitting back in the dressing room and Bill went over and got the mandolin out of the case and sat there and played on it for a little

while, and he said, 'Yeah, I like this mandolin. I need to get one of these.'"
As Red Henry claims, Monroe "said it sounded more like his old F-5 than
any other mandolin he'd ever played."

But Bill Monroe would have to wait. Not only had Randy already found a
buyer for the first mandolin but he had also received an order for a second.
Randy sold mandolin #1 to a friend and fellow luthier, Bernie Michelle, reportedly for $750. Incidentally, Randy has frequently fielded the question
of whether or not he regrets selling his original creation. "I look at things
like that a little different than other people," he told the *Savannah Morning
News*. "I always figure I can build another one. I can't print money, but I
can always build another one of those" (Roseberry 1998).

Randy Wood #2

Randy had begun construction on mandolin #2 when Roland White paid
him a visit. White had just been recruited to play in Lester Flatt's new
band following the breakup of Flatt and Scruggs, and he needed a better
instrument. He asked if Randy could build him an instrument like mandolin #1. Randy responded affirmatively and agreed to sell mandolin #2 to
White once it was completed. When White first played the instrument, he
connected with it immediately. "I loved it right away," White remembers.
"It was just fantastic. It was the closest thing that I had ever had to real-
sounding old F-5."

Randy was more concerned about White's liking the instrument than
securing a quick sale. He let White take #2 home and play it for a while to
be sure it was satisfactory, but there was little doubt in White's mind that
he would keep the mandolin. "I called him up and asked, 'How much do
you want for it?'" They negotiated a deal for White to exchange some cash
and a guitar in return for Randy Wood #2. "I think I gave him the guitar
and $250."

While Randy Wood #2 is a close facsimile of #1, Randy Wood #2 is recognizable for its offset "The Gibson" logo on the headstock. The logo is
positioned far enough left of center that the top tuner peg pierces the "G."
On Gibson-built headstocks, or on other Randy Wood headstocks, for that
matter, the tuners do not encroach on the letters. That logo placement is

now one of the defining features of Randy's second mandolin, along with its symmetric twenty-fret fingerboard.

The mandolin was White's primary instrument for much of his career, which gave Randy's product wide exposure to bluegrass audiences. He played it until 2004. When White prepared to publish a biography of his late brother, Clarence, he sold the mandolin to raise money for printing.

White still speaks of the instrument with pride, saying, "I listen to recordings that I've done with it, and it just spoke out so well. I mean, when I touched it, it told me what I wanted to hear. That's the way I see it. It suited me just fine, and I played a lot of other mandolins. I mean a lot of people couldn't believe that it wasn't a real Gibson, that it wasn't an old Loar, only that 'The Gibson' was in the wrong place."

Randy Wood #3

After honoring his commitments to the buyers of #1 and #2, Randy built #3 for Monroe. Other fledgling builders might have caved under pressure when the Father of Bluegrass requested one of their first instruments, but Randy believed in fairness, even if it meant he had to tell someone as well known as Monroe to wait in line for his turn.

As with #1 and #2, it takes a discerning eye to differentiate #3 from a Gibson F-5. All three mimic the swooping body lines and sunburst finish of a Gibson model. But the pearl inlay of the vase on Randy's headstock is lower than the inlay on the Gibson models. And the tuner pegs on the Gibson version form two parallel rows of four pegs each, while the two rows on #3 converge slightly toward the nut.

When Randy completed the instrument, he gave it to Monroe as a gift, although he claims Monroe was more than willing to pay for it. But Randy felt indebted to Monroe because he had begun sending some of his instruments to Randy for repairs. "That was the only instrument I have ever given to a star, but he had done a lot for me during the early years," Randy told reporter Dan Lowery (2000a).

Randy's reputation as a luthier gained additional credibility once Monroe began playing Randy's mandolin on stages across the country. Monroe also lent the mandolin to Marty Stuart, who was going to work for

Lester Flatt after Roland White left the band. Much like his predecessor in Flatt's band, Stuart lacked a quality instrument for his new job. Monroe lent Stuart Randy Wood #3, and Stuart played it for three and a half years. Red Henry believes that due to the exposure from Monroe, White, and Stuart, "people were seeing that these Randy Wood mandolins sounded so good, and they all said 'The Gibson' on them. I think Randy was selling mandolins for Gibson right then instead of for himself."

Mandolin #3 evokes memorable stories from both Roland White and Red Henry. After Marty Stuart gave #3 back to Monroe, Roland White called Monroe and asked if he could borrow the mandolin for a few days. White's #2 was in Randy's shop for a repair, and White needed an instrument for some scheduled shows. As White recalls, he phoned Monroe with the request, and Monroe was glad to lend it—on one condition: "Just don't forget where you got it." Once White received #2 from Randy, he tried to reach Monroe to return #3, but Monroe never seemed to be available for the hand-off. Instead, Monroe repeatedly told White, "You hang onto it. I don't have a good place to keep it." White held on to #3 and continued to play it. Several months later, White received a call from a frantic Monroe, who said, "I've got a mandolin missing!" White asked, "Are we talking about the Randy Wood one?" Monroe confirmed that was the one, and White laughed, telling Monroe, "I've been trying to return it to you!" He did so, and Monroe kept it for the rest of his life.

Today, the #3 mandolin belongs to Red Henry, the owner of #1. He acquired the mandolin through an unusual twist of fate that has a lot to do with Randy's decision to copy the Gibson branding on his early mandolins. "Bill passed away, and finally, in December 2001, was his estate sale," Henry recalls. "So I found out it was going on and got a copy of the sale lots listing, because for years I had heard Bill Monroe had Randy Wood #3. And I had #1, and I liked it. I had played #2, and I liked it. I thought, *Wouldn't it be cool to get a Bill Monroe mandolin?*" Henry grew disappointed as he examined the auction listings. He did not see a Randy Wood mandolin among the items. "So I gave up."

But Henry's wife, Murphy, did not concede so easily. Unbeknownst to Red, she called his uncle, John Hedgecoth (who was working at Gruhn

Guitars, just a few blocks from the Country Music Hall of Fame, where the auction was held) and asked him to find out if any one of the instruments on auction preview was actually Randy Wood #3. Hedgecoth walked over to inspect the items at the Hall of Fame. One instrument caught his eye. The auction catalog listed it as "an old Gibson mandolin," but Hedgecoth boasts, "One look, and I knew it was Randy's work. And the label said, '003,' I think, and 'Gibson by Randy Wood.'" Hedgecoth and Murphy Henry attended the auction and waited eagerly for the bidding to begin. "They got to this mandolin, and this guy got up and gave a disclaimer and said, 'This is actually not a Gibson mandolin,'" Hedgecoth recounts. The crowd expressed a collective sigh of disappointment, "except for us. We said, 'yeah!'" Murphy Henry won the bid for Randy Wood #3 and presented it to Red as a Christmas present.

Henry speaks about his Randy Wood mandolins like a father speaks about his children, loving both while embracing their differences, saying about #3, "It's got a completely different tone than #1 or #2," Henry says. He further elaborates:

> [Number Three's] tone has a lot of mid-range. It has an amazing amount of volume. And it has the classic projection. It's got as good a projection as any instrument I've ever known. One time we went out to play a local gig, and my friend Dave McLaughlin went with us to play guitar. Before we started, I had to go to the car to get something, and he was sitting in this party tent with the mandolin, playing Randy Wood #3, and I went back to the car and got something out of it and started walking back. I must have been 150 feet away and thought how much that mandolin was coming through. I walked all the way from back there to ten feet away, and the apparent volume stayed exactly the same. It seems to violate the laws of physics, but I've heard of some amazing projecting instruments that can do that—that will sound the same a hundred feet away as ten feet away. This one did.

Henry also praises the playability of Randy Wood #3. Early in his lutherie career, Randy understood the qualities that players value. They are not necessarily the aesthetics that collectors might particularly appreciate, and the qualities are often subjective. But Henry hinted at those qualities, saying:

> Randy Wood #3—it's just so solid, a very consistent performer. It stays in tune very well, and it also has a particularly, I think, higher than average arch in the top and back. I can hear it when I play it better than any other mandolin I've got. You know, most musical instruments project all of their sound out front, but the people in front of it will hear it a lot better than the person who's playing it. Randy Wood #3 you can hear real well on stage. People playing on stage can hear it. I can hear it, which makes it an exceptionally good mandolin for that kind of work.

Randy's talents as a luthier were becoming evident through the exposure of his first three mandolins, but self-promotion has never been his forte. To gain the exposure necessary to set the hook in this fledgling career, he would need an injection of some business acumen into his repair and construction activity. Little did he know a young snake collector from Chicago would provide the infusion.

5

GTR

It was pure magic to have Norman Blake there in our
little office/studio and to be able to go back and forth from
our shop and the backstage area of the Johnny Cash TV show
and meet world-class musicians . . . but I also recall that there
were some days when we took in as little as $5 for
the entire day's proceeds.

GEORGE GRUHN

George Gruhn

If there were ever an unlikely colleague of Randy Wood's, it would be George Gruhn. While Randy tended farms in rural Georgia, Gruhn spent his childhood years in New York, Pittsburgh, and then Chicago. As a teenager, Gruhn was slight of build with glasses and flowing dark hair—a striking contrast to the rugged yet neatly groomed Randy Wood. But in the late 1960s, George, Randy, and Tut Taylor found themselves in comparable communities of musical instrument enthusiasts. With Tut as the elder statesman and social connector for the unlikely threesome, the trio founded a pioneering vintage guitar retail shop, known as GTR, in the heart of Nashville. The threesome did not remain intact long, but in that short time, something special began. As Neil Rosenberg explains in *Bluegrass* (1985), "Although there had long been bluegrass bands in [Nashville], never before had an infrastructure existed. In 1970 this started to change when GTR, Inc., an instrument sales and repair shop specializing in the old acoustic instruments sought by bluegrass musicians, was opened by dealer George Gruhn, collector-musician Tut Taylor, and re-pairman Randy Wood."

Randy found musical instruments at the intersection of two of his passions: playing music and woodworking. George Gruhn arrived on the instrument scene by way of his own passion—collecting snakes. Gruhn's father was a pathologist at the Skokie Valley Hospital north of Chicago, and George showed a strong academic inclination from an early age, thirsting for deep knowledge on subjects that interested him. That drive, combined with an eye for detail and an indifference to social norms, pro-pelled Gruhn to pursue his interests to extreme ends. Herpetology, the study of reptiles, particularly enthralled him. George was fascinated by the variety of creatures in that class. He relished learning how to spot the subtleties distinguishing one species from another. He loved paging through the Audubon field guides categorizing animals according to their visible features. His academic interest went beyond what he saw in books; he collected snakes as pets, too. In the 1960s he was also influenced by the growing folk music scene. He discovered guitars, much like the snakes he collected, could be found in a wide array of shapes, sizes, and colors. While Gruhn has long enjoyed playing stringed instruments, he also ap-proached them with the mind of a zoological taxonomist. Gruhn viewed instruments as species of animals just waiting for an organized observer to catalog them according to their unique features, just as John James Audubon had cataloged birds he studied in the early 1800s.

Collecting snakes and guitars became more than hobbies for Gruhn. They became his obsessions. Finding the rare species of snake or guitar was the ultimate thrill. The rarer they were, the more the pursuit fasci-nated him. But as his guitar collection grew, he realized the guitars he coveted were hard to find. "While I was a student at the University of Chicago, I scoured classified ads in the newspapers, checked the bulletin boards at the school, and visited pawnshops and music stores," Gruhn re-members. "But truly fine vintage instruments were few and far between" (*Gruhn Newsletter* #11 2003). Gruhn learned, as did Randy, that older in-struments were built with a level of craftsmanship that diminished after World War II, as mass-production methods infiltrated guitar factories struggling to keep up with growing demand. His zeal for rare vintage pieces often required creative thinking to secure a trade. "One time, there was a bulletin board posting, somebody had a Martin 000-18 made in 1926," Gruhn recalls about his discovery of this prized guitar model. I traded them an eight-foot boa constrictor—with cage—and fifty dollars! He was happy. I was happy. Hopefully the boa constrictor was happy."

A glimpse into George's apartment during his upper-class years in college would have revealed what mattered most to him. "I filled up a good bit of my room with a small bed, guitar cases and snake cages," Gruhn says. He was studying animal psychology and in particular the feeding behaviors of pit vipers. In support of his studies, he filled the department lab with cages housing his subjects. "After a few months there, the department chairman objected because his wife was afraid of them, and I was told I had to remove them. So I took them to my apartment."

As Gruhn fell deeper into his passion for collecting guitars, he found himself fantasizing about Nashville. Recalling his perceptions of the Music City, Gruhn says, "I figured that there'd be guitars hanging from the trees, and I was going to be able to score all kinds of neat stuff if I'd just come from Chicago to Nashville." In short, he says, "I figured Nashville would be where the guitars were." In the summer of 1966 he decided to go looking for the "neat stuff." In retrospect he confesses, "That was not a very well-informed decision. Chicago was where the money was in the old days—at least one of the places—and the South was not. And Chicago also was a hotbed of guitar activity for country, and blues, and jazz, and pop, and all sorts of music. Much more so wide-based than Nashville would have been." But this is a conclusion reached after years of reflection. To the young George Gruhn, Nashville beckoned.

Gruhn drove down to Nashville that summer, but what he found disappointed him. "I went into Hank Snow's store, and I found one music teacher who had an early-1930s Gibson L-12, but there wasn't much else. There was no vintage stuff at that store, and he didn't know anything about finding vintage, either." His next stop was Sho-Bud, the downtown music shop founded by Nashville heavyweights Shot Jackson and Buddy Emmons. He found guitars, but he was nonplussed to find that few people there shared his reverence for originality. "They had a complete repair shop on their third floor devoted to mutilating guitars. Anything that they touched was the reverse Midas touch: they touch it, and it turns to shit." He elaborates, "They couldn't leave well enough alone. They thought everything needed to be refinished, and it was great if they had big Lester Flatt-style pickguards [covering original wood finishes], and they were more interested in hot-rodding and customizing guitars." Jackson and Emmons were likely responding to customer demand. Many musicians *wanted* to have guitars like the one Lester Flatt played. "Nashville artists at that time took their guitars there to be customized and refinished," Gruhn admits. He nevertheless concludes, "There was just no respect for them."

Undeterred, Gruhn next visited Hewgley's. "They didn't have anything I wanted," but the store manager, Jim Broadus, told him, "There really isn't anything much in this town that you're going to find, but there's a guy down in Chattanooga, and his name is Mike Longworth, who has a bunch of old Martins and just the kind of stuff that you seem to want." Broadus handed Gruhn a business card with Longworth's telephone number and address.

"Well, I've driven all the way from Chicago, and here I am. Um, how long does it take to get to Chattanooga?" George asked.

"About four hours," Broadus replied.

George got back in his car and headed southeast for Chattanooga, finally arriving around dinner time. He called the number Jim Broadus gave him, and Sue Longworth answered the phone. "She and Mike hadn't been married very long at that point," Gruhn explains, "and she said he was out of town. He was off in Asheville, North Carolina, at some kind of a fiddling festival." She invited Gruhn to come over and look at her husband's guitars anyway. "He had a stash of pearl-trimmed Martins and other sorts of neat stuff, which was highly appealing to me." Gruhn asked her what was so special about this meeting in Asheville.

"People come from all over and they have picking, and trading instruments and everything," she replied.

"Well, that's probably where I ought to be," Gruhn told her. "How far is that?"

"About four hours."

So George saddled up again and navigated the dark, winding two-lane mountain roads to Asheville. "I arrived at about one in the morning. And I pulled up to this shopping-center-strip-mall parking lot area." What he saw thrilled him. "There were people with all kinds of neat instruments, and they picked 'til dawn. There were original flat-head five-string banjos and everything else you could think of. It was all right there. There were guys playing real Loar F-5s." Gruhn wasted little time finding Mike Longworth. "I didn't even know what Mike looked like, but I recognized what a prewar D-45 looked like. I just walked up to him and said, 'Hi, I'm George. You must be Mike. I was over at your house this evening and your wife gave me the directions on how to get here.'" One can only imagine Longworth's reaction to hearing such news from a young stranger.

George Gruhn had finally discovered what he left Chicago to find. The festival attendees were playing the old prewar instruments he coveted. Additionally, he found the festivals were natural marketplaces where trading took place. Gruhn did not engage in much trading at his first festival, but it inspired him nonetheless. "It certainly introduced me to what was going on, and it was just great!" he exclaims. While at Asheville, George would also learn about the burgeoning bluegrass festival circuit, and he followed it to other venues, such as Galax, Virginia, and Union Grove, North Carolina.

George, Tut, and Randy Meet over Snakes

Tut Taylor also happened to be in attendance at Asheville that year. Guitarist Norman Blake, a longtime friend of Taylor's, once said, "Tut has always been there, right in the middle of things" (Johnson 2011), and it took no time for Tut to get acquainted with this intriguing newcomer. The first meeting between George and Tut was uneventful, but in the course of introductions, George disclosed his passion for snakes. When George showed up to Asheville the following year with some of his scaly companions in tow, Tut begged to see them.

That year, 1967, Randy accompanied Tut to Asheville. Upon arrival, Randy must have been perplexed by Tut's eagerness to see this kid from

Chicago. Gruhn remembers, "Tut wanted to see the snakes, so I remember quite well that I took the suitcase to his motel room and just opened it up on the bed, spreading out copperheads, cottonmouths, and timber rattlesnakes all over the bed. He knew that I said that they were perfectly tame, but he didn't believe it until he could see it, but I just spread them out on the bed and just handled them where they'd just crawl up my arm." (Gruhn acknowledges he has a certain knack for handling snakes. "I don't have any trouble handling them, and they like me just fine. But very few people want to do that, and that's probably best. If you do have an accident with one of them, it's very messy," he says.)

Gruhn devised an ingenious inventory protection plan, thanks to his comfort around animals most people found terrifying. Tut recalls, "George kept a snake in the guitar case. The thing about it is, you didn't know which guitar case it was. So he didn't have to worry about anybody bothering his stuff." Tut was clearly impressed with Gruhn's clever tactic. Of course, the bluegrass festival season peaked during the summer months, and Gruhn's snakes would not survive locked in a guitar case for hours in the trunk of his car in the hot Southern sun. But George was astute enough to understand the strength of most people's aversion to the reptiles. He hid snakes in a random guitar case only during the spring, when temperatures were not too hot. "But once word got out," Gruhn says, "nobody messed with my car."

Gruhn's Sour Deal

Tut and George cemented their friendship in Asheville when Tut helped George in the wake of a bad trade. As George remembers, "I did a really lousy trade. I'd always wanted a good F-5 Loar, and I ended up with what turned out to be a forgery. Tut was there, and he pretty much clued me in that I'd been screwed." Tut recalls, "He come to me one day, smiling from ear to ear. He had been wanting an F-5 bad. Well, he got one in Asheville, and he couldn't wait to show it to me, and when he did, I looked at it and said, 'George, this is not original.' I thought George was almost going to cry." Tut knew George had been fooled, and he was sympathetic. "He had been taken, you know. It's not a great feeling." Tut was almost twenty years older than George, and he watched George through experienced eyes. "I kinda felt sorry for George a lot," he says. "He was just coming into the instrument game and didn't know anything."

The bad trade was conducted with a restaurateur from nearby Morganton, North Carolina. Tut decided to right the wrong. It was, of course, a delicate matter to accuse someone of dealing a fake with the hopes of reversing the deal and coming out alive. It required tact and local knowledge, two things George was short on in those days. "Ol' George, bless his heart," Tut chuckles. "He was a Yankee at heart, one hundred percent." Meanwhile, Randy was observing all of this from the sidelines. Randy, like Tut, knew George hardly stood a chance of reversing the deal by himself against a rural Appalachian. "George was a little ol' skinny, runty college kid. He wasn't going to face up to a bunch of damn mountaineers." Even George confesses he was green. "At that point I was young, inexperienced, and Yankee." Tut and George found the local sheriff's office and sat in the waiting area until a deputy could see them. Tut recalls, "I told George, 'You sit in this seat and don't you say a damn word. Don't you even open your mouth!' He was the kind of fellow back then that just about everything he said would offend somebody."

But George had something working in his favor. He was attending graduate school at the Duke University zoological department, so he would remain in North Carolina. Tut talked with the deputy, who knew the man at the restaurant, and Tut persuaded the deputy to talk to the man about reversing the trade. According to Gruhn, the deputy only agreed to help because Tut could honestly assure him that George would be living in North Carolina and would be responsive to any potential legal proceedings that might develop. The deputy went out on his mission while George and Tut waited in the sheriff's office. To their delight, the deputy returned and told them to go see the man and get their instruments back. "So we did," Tut boasts. "The guy was awful upset, but he had no choice." Tut took pride in wielding his experience and local knowledge to help a newbie, and George was immensely grateful. "Tut and I certainly became much better friends after that."

Vintage Instrument Trading as a Business

The summers George spent on the bluegrass festival circuit impacted him in two significant ways. First, he unearthed the deposits of vintage instruments he traveled south to find. They were not exactly "hanging from the trees" in Nashville, as he had originally imagined, but he found them on the festival circuit through nuanced negotiating tactics he was quickly learning from Tut and others. Gruhn proved to be a quick study, because the second impact of the festivals was the spread of his reputation for having an impressive vintage instrument collection. As a result, his trading activity picked up considerably while he was still ostensibly pursuing a career in academics. In 1968, now as a graduate student studying animal behavior in the psychology department at the University of Tennessee in Knoxville, he was approached by Hank Williams Jr., who was an avid collector of vintage instruments, too.

Williams pitched the idea that a move from Knoxville to Nashville might be advantageous for Gruhn. "Hank told me that Nashville had no one like me and that I ought to move to town. He said that if I wanted to come he would have an apartment waiting for me and would help me set up a music store." The idea sounded appealing to Gruhn. He acknowledges, "While I enjoyed studying feeding behavior of pit vipers, it was quite evident that I would probably not make a good living doing that" (*Gruhn Newsletter* #11 2003). George dropped out of graduate school before completing his PhD, and he moved to Nashville. Initially Williams supported George by buying guitars from his collection. But the music store plans never materialized.

As George committed himself to trading instruments full-time, he found himself in need of an instrument repairman. A collector's greatest discoveries were often those underappreciated instruments that had suffered decades of neglect, usually in an attic of some descendant of the original owner. The instruments might need anything from new frets to patched holes to make them appealing to another buyer. Many owners of these instruments assumed the old Martins and Gibsons were junk. George knew better, and he knew whom to call to bring them back to life. "As an active dealer of vintage instruments, I needed a good repairman to service and restore the instruments I found," George writes. "Unfortunately there were none in Nashville to suit me. Randy Wood was located in Muscle Shoals, Alabama, about two hours from Nashville.... I used to go down every two weeks carrying a load of instruments to be repaired and picking up whatever was ready." Between Gruhn's repair work and Wood's own projects, "Randy was up to his eyeballs in work." Nashville had repair shops, to be sure, but George struggled to find repairmen in town who cared to preserve the original craftsmanship in old instruments. As George had noticed on his first trip to Nashville, "Shot Jackson had the very best of intentions and had extremely good relations with the Nashville country-western players, but he just never developed any understanding of the vintage market." In Randy Wood, he found a capable repairman who appreciated the craftsmanship inherent in Gruhn's prized vintage instruments (*Gruhn Newsletter* #12 2003).

The Gibson Contract

Music City had lured George away from academia, and it was exerting a similar pull on Tut and Randy. "Tut for years had wanted to move to Nashville," Randy remembers. Tut, the consummate networker, found an angle to realize that dream. "In late '69, Tut was in contact with Gibson, or I think they contacted him, or something, trying to find me, or that's what Tut said anyway," Randy says, fully aware Tut knew what buttons to push to get Randy's attention. Gibson expressed a desire to kick-start some of their acoustic product line by reintroducing the Florentine and All-American banjos, with necks carved by Randy Wood and resonator backs painted by Tut Taylor. Randy's reputation for artistry had been growing because of the work he and Rual were procuring at festivals, and Tut's reputation for painting had been well established through his career painting signs. Randy explains that "Tut got in touch with me and wanted to know if I would be interested in moving to Nashville and opening up a music store, using this Gibson thing as a ready-made way to make money." Tut knew Gruhn had moved to Nashville with the frustrated intentions of opening a music store, so he contacted George to gauge his interest in joining forces. After all three had discussed the idea, they drove to the Gibson headquarters in Kalamazoo, Michigan, in the fall of 1969 to clarify the terms of their engagement with Gibson representatives.

Anticipation must have been palpable on that road trip, because they effectively agreed to open a shop together, regardless of the outcome of the meeting with Gibson. Randy remembers, "On the drive up there and the drive back, we pretty much decided, no matter what, that we were going to go ahead and open up a store in Nashville and deal in vintage instruments. Nobody was doing that at the time, and we felt like there was a big demand for that."

The three met with Gibson's president, Stan Rendell. At first, the meeting outcome seemed promising. "Gibson actually sent us down a spindle carving machine," George explains. "It would carve two copies at once, and we could carve necks and resonators, so we experimented a bit to see, because we didn't have a contract yet so far as pricing and everything." After Tut and Randy tried their hand at carving and painting some samples, Gibson clued them into the pricing plan. "It turned out that Gibson only wanted to pay ninety dollars for the heel carving and painting," according to George. "Well, they were going to sell those banjos, even back then, for close to four thousand dollars list! And they were going to pay us ninety bucks to do the work!" he says with exasperation. "It didn't pay; you'd lose money. So our relationship with Gibson pretty well ended." But the possibility of a deal with Gibson had already enticed Tut and Randy to relocate to be closer to the action in the music business. Randy, Irene, and their young daughter, Renee, uprooted once again and moved to Nashville.

GTR Is Born

George Gruhn, Tut Taylor, and Randy Wood had arrived in Nashville, but once the Gibson deal fell through, their plans were far from certain. It was an especially risky move for Tut and Randy. "It was a major move for all of us. For Tut it involved closing his business in Milledgeville and moving his sizable family to Nashville for a less than totally secure future. For Randy it involved moving from Muscle Shoals to Nashville for the new venture," says Gruhn, the only bachelor of the three at that time (*Gruhn Newsletter* #12 2003).

For George, Tut, and Randy, any trepidation gave way to the excitement of opening a new style of music shop: a place where the age and quality of the products were valued over the sheen of newness. "There were virtually no guitar specialty shops and virtually no vintage instrument dealers with the exception of Lundberg Stringed Instruments in Berkeley, California, Fretted Instruments in Greenwich Village in New York City, and the Fret Shop in Chicago near the university I attended," Gruhn says.

While Music Row was buzzing with recording activity, downtown Nashville in 1969 had plenty of available retail space, assuming the potential tenant approached his neighbors with an open mind. It did not take long for the three to find a building. Randy says, "As soon as we got back from Kalamazoo, George started looking for a building that we could rent." George elaborates:

> We found a building housing a rundown restaurant on 4th Avenue right off the corner of Broadway. Although we put down a deposit on rent, we soon found that the restaurant owner did not, in fact, own the building, nor did she have a long-term lease. While our deposit went down the tubes after it became clear that the building owner would not give us lease terms that were acceptable, fortunately we were not out much, and the building directly next door at 111 4th Avenue North was available.... It wasn't much of a place. It measured 20' × 60' total and was in poor condition, but Tut and Randy quickly set to work to build walls dividing the building into a showroom, a small office and a workshop. Out of the total 20' × 60' only the first 15' plus large bay windows were devoted to the showroom. The office area ... measured only 10' × 10'. The rest was devoted to the repair shop. (*Gruhn Newsletter* #12 2003)

Gruhn's assessment that "it wasn't much of a place" may be generous. He says, "Each spring, termites swarmed out of the wood" in the building. "The instruments were safe because the insects wanted moist wood." Rent for the building was initially $125 per month. Randy admits that this was a lot of money in the eyes of the three men trying to start a business. But Randy also concedes, "In the scheme of things, it wasn't all that much money. And it was a fair-sized building. It faced Fourth Avenue." One of its most desirable features was that it was in the same block as the *Opry*. Emphasizing the proximity, Randy says, the back door of their building "almost opened up to the *Opry* back door. There was a forty or fifty yard difference between the two." There were less desirable neighbors, too. "We had an adult movie house on one side, and there was, I think, a loan company on the other side." George says there were nearby porn shops and massage parlors "that would massage every part of the body."

The new store needed a name. According to Randy, "All the way back from Kalamazoo we had been trying to think of a name for the thing. Somebody suggested, well, why don't we use our initials for that. Then we realized that if we arranged them that way, GTR, then it was also short for 'guitar.'" The name has misled some observers into believing all three men were partners in the store. However, George and Tut were the only owners. Randy was employed as the repairman. Although Randy did not own stock, the GTR name gives him rightful credit for his significant role in the formation of the new shop.

Each of the three men brought his own possessions to build the store's opening inventory. Randy explains, "George probably had a hundred instruments or more. George was living in a three-room apartment, and two of the rooms were jam packed with instruments. I took some tools, and I had to build some, such as fretboard sanding blocks and single-handle spoke carvers, and I bought some. And Tut had some equipment." GTR opened its doors to the public in January 1970.

George and Tut remembered some of their early inventory and how inexpensive it seemed by current standards. "I still remember vividly that when we opened the doors we had a beautiful 1938 herringbone D-28 Martin priced at $800 and a 1946 herringbone D for $600," Gruhn recalls. "They were not quick, easy sellers. I also remember a squeaky-clean 1959 dot inlay ES-335 we sold in 1970 for what was then top dollar at $400. Needless to say today's prices are much higher" (*Gruhn Newsletter* #11 2003). "Little did we know!" Tut exclaims, recognizing that the same instruments today would fetch many thousands of dollars. "And we liked to never have sold them!" Vintage instruments may have harbored latent value, but it was a tough sell to much of the public. Most buyers were not willing to pay for the value that George and Tut saw in their instruments. In a retrospective newsletter to customers, Gruhn recounts a time when he proudly placed a turn-of-the-century three-point Gibson scroll-model mandolin in the GTR display window. In front of the instrument was a sign that read, "Mandolin, handmade by Orville Gibson, circa 1900." George writes, "I still vividly remember sitting in the showroom talking with Tut and Randy when an elderly couple came tottering up to the window and squinted down at the mandolin. One said, 'Look honey, there's a fiddle.' The other said, 'I wonder how much it costs?' Next came 'The sign says $19' and then 'Aw, that's too much, let's go'" (*Gruhn Newsletter* #12 2003).

The shop reflected the unique personalities of George, Tut, and Randy. Tut, the sign painter by trade, hand-painted placards for instrument displays in the showroom. George brought his animals into the mix. "George had a pet parrot he kept in a cage," Tut recalls. George was careful to keep the parrot contained, but a later employee, Bernie Michelle, let the parrot out of the cage one evening. The bird ate a hole in a Gibson ES-150 guitar consigned by one of Nashville's top session guitarists, Harold Bradley. As a result, Michelle was forced to buy the guitar. Randy kept his repair shop in a condition that would become familiar to all who know him: cluttered. George remembers Randy's shop benches were buried under so much stuff "you'd have to go through thirty feet of counter space looking for a tool."

Famous Musicians at GTR

GTR built a reputation as a premier source of vintage instruments, but in its early days, one of its most important assets was its proximity to the Ryman Auditorium. The Ryman attracted crowds of music lovers and performers—just the kind of people that appreciate vintage instruments—to downtown Nashville and to the sidewalks fronting the newly opened GTR. In 1970, the *Johnny Cash Show* was filmed in the Ryman. That show brought not only fans but world-class musicians through the doors of GTR. Norman Blake, a now-legendary bluegrass flat-pick guitarist and songwriter, played in the show's house band. Despite the enviable gig, Blake needed to supplement his income by teaching guitar lessons. During downtime between rehearsals next door at the Ryman, Blake visited GTR, and he befriended George, Tut, and Randy. Tut and Randy built a wall to form a room in the back of their building where Blake could give lessons. Gruhn explains, "We covered the walls with egg cartons inside—that was our soundproofing—and that was his teaching studio. We charged zero commission." They knew having a steady stream of students would bring traffic to the store. It was a win-win scenario, and the generosity that they showed Blake turned him into a lifelong friend of all three.

The *Cash Show* indirectly drew music celebrities into GTR, since the music variety show featured different musical stars each week. Rehearsals for the show would begin on Monday mornings and would continue through Wednesdays, with the practice sessions culminating in a dress rehearsal on Wednesday nights. Filming for the show took place on Thursdays. "So Monday, Tuesday, and Wednesday, whoever was going to be there that week had to be there," Randy says. "But they probably didn't have to do anything but thirty minutes or an hour out of a day, but the other seven hours, they were there. And they didn't want to hang out in the Ryman." One reason they did not want to hang out in the Ryman was that it lacked air conditioning. To accommodate the musical guests, the *Cash Show* rented the upstairs portion of Roy Acuff's air-conditioned downtown office for the musicians' use. In the evenings, these musicians had become accustomed to relaxing in the back rooms of Tootsie's Orchid Lounge, which shared the alley next to the Ryman. But GTR offered a new alternative during daylight hours.

GTR developed an appealing vibe. In a matter of a couple of months, GTR was differentiating itself as a guitar shop without sales pressure—a place where people who just wanted to *be* around guitars were as welcome as paying customers. "We did have a lot of nice instruments," Randy admits, "and most of the stars enjoyed vintage and high-end instruments, but there was only us and Sho-Bud, and Sho-Bud was so commercial. They would all go there, because it was Sho-Bud, after all. But they enjoyed more coming over to our place and hanging out." The freedom to hang out was crucial. When musicians hang out with instruments around them, a breakout jam session is inevitable. Randy boasts, "We usually had some good pickers hanging out in the store all the time." It is a description that would be apt for all of Randy's work spaces.

The Bobby Whitlock Fingerboard

One good picker who found his way to GTR the first year was Bobby Whitlock, who performed on the *Cash Show* alongside Eric Clapton in Derek and the Dominos. The group was steeped in the traditions of the blues, but their appearance was decidedly hip for 1970. Whitlock wandered into GTR during the week leading up to the *Cash Show's* filming, and an inlaid fingerboard caught his eye. Randy enjoyed designing and creating mother-of-pearl inlays on guitar fingerboards, and when the demand for repair work was light, he filled his time with his own inlay projects. On one particular fingerboard, he embellished the usual domino-like pattern of dots with an intricate vine, upon which the shimmering letters "RW" were centered. As Wood explains, "I put my initials in the middle of it, for lack of anything better to do to put in there, and it lay in the front window of the store so people walking by could see it.

"On a Wednesday, this guy came in—hippie looking guy—and wanted to know if that fingerboard was for sale," Randy recalls. George Gruhn, tending the counter, responded affirmatively. That hippie looking guy wanted to know if the fingerboard could be installed on his guitar by the next day. Randy remembers telling him, "Ain't no way that I can do that! I'd have to saw the pearl out, and inlay it and engrave it and refret the guitar." This potential customer clarified his request. He did not want a fingerboard *like* that one; he wanted *that* one. "I explained to him that it had my initials in it, so it wouldn't do him any good," Randy continues. The man replied, "Those are my initials, too. My name is Robert Whitlock." Randy acknowledges, "Everybody called him Bobby, and then it dawned on me who he was." Randy stayed up most of that night, gluing and refretting Whitlock's D-35 with the new fingerboard. "Whether he used it on the *Cash Show* I have no idea," Wood says. "But at least he had it." That fingerboard graced the cover of Whitlock's 1972 self-titled album, and he continues to play and record with it today.

Clapton's Guitars

Whitlock's bandmate, Eric Clapton, also wandered into GTR and found plenty to pique his interest. In an August 1976 issue of *Guitar Player*, Clapton responded to interviewer Dan Forte's question about specialty guitars he owned: "I've got a wood-body Dobro with a Martin-type neck, reworked by Randy Wood. I got it at George Gruhn's shop in Nashville." An Eric Clapton fan website elaborates on this instrument with the following description: "Wood decorated the guitar with the vintage Martin style torch inlay on the headstock, style 45 abalone inlay on the body and a 'tree of life' inlay on the fingerboard complete with Eric's name. 16 years later, this guitar made what was probably its first public appearance during the 'Unplugged' session at Bray Studios and then became a stage regular for acoustic slide blues during the 90's blues period" (ClaptonWeb .com). Clapton claims that GTR was pivotal in introducing him to Dobro-style guitars. In the lot notes for the Crossroads Guitar Auction held by Christie's in 2004, Clapton explains how he fell in love with the instruments after seeing one owned by Duane Allman. "His was the first one I ever saw, it came from GTR. . . . So I went to GTR. . . . They made a custom guitar for me and . . . whenever I've seen a blonde wooden top Dobro that resembled my first one . . . I'd buy it because they're very rare . . . very, very unusual and usually they're very well made, and they sound good—so I've collected them" (Crossroads Guitar Auction Lot Notes 2004). Clapton brought the Dobro to mainstream audiences through such songs as "Let It Grow," "My Father's Eyes," and several tracks from his Grammy-winning *Unplugged* album. GTR brought the Dobro to Clapton.

Clapton's purchases at GTR did not stop with Dobros. He also bought a 1968 Martin 000–28 "in Nashville from GTR in 1970 and later used it for a lengthy period extending from 1974's *461 Ocean Boulevard* through his 1994–95 *Nothing but the Blues* tour," according to an 2015 article in *Guitar Aficionado*.

Of all of Clapton's guitars, perhaps the most famous one can also trace its roots back to GTR. George Gruhn, quoted in a published interview in the *University of Chicago Magazine*, claimed:

> Eric Clapton came to the store in 1970 or '71. . . . He had been a Gibson player but had become a big fan of Fender Stratocasters—which were not as popular or expensive as they are today—and he bought a number of them to give to friends, including ex-Beatle George Harrison. But he bought a number of '50s and '60s models from my store and a lot of Strat parts from another store down the street, taking the best parts from all the guitars to assemble his beloved "Blackie," Clapton's main guitar until his brief retirement from music in the late 1980s. (Makos 1996)

Elvis Presley Inlay

While at GTR, Randy Wood completed what is likely his most widely viewed piece—the personalized fingerboard on the black Gibson Dove that Elvis Presley played in the 1970s. The guitar was later put up for auction, and according to the lot notes provided by Graceland, "Elvis wielded this iconic instrument in dozens and dozens of concerts from November 1971 until September 1973 and then again in July of 1975, before famously handing it to a fan in the front row one night in Asheville, North Carolina. The Ebony Dove was the most photographed and widely seen of any of Elvis' guitars as he played it during the January 1973 *Aloha from Hawaii via Satellite* concert broadcast."

The guitar was a gift to Elvis from his father for achieving black belt status in karate, and Randy was tapped to personalize the guitar with a mother-of-pearl inlay on the fingerboard. Like most of Randy's inlay projects, he first sketched his idea on paper. The design consists of Elvis Presley's name in script letters, the "E" and "P" embellished with curls resembling thorns on a rose stem. Randy then went to work placing the letters between the third and fourteenth frets. He accomplished the project with little fanfare in his workshop. Little did it matter to him that the customer was one of the most famous men on the planet.

Merle Travis and the Water-Soaked Neck Repair

Vintage instruments often surfaced after years of varying degrees of neglect or abuse. GTR needed salable inventory, so George and Tut scoured the market to add to the collection, and Randy stayed busy bringing guitars, mandolins, and banjos back to life. Finding old neglected instruments, repairing them, and convincing a fledgling market that they were valuable was the bread-and-butter work that put GTR on the map. Sometimes an instrument might simply need a new set of strings to revive it. At other times Randy would have to perform more invasive procedures, such as disassembling an instrument to realign a warped neck. According to luthier and instrument historian Roger Siminoff, "These guys were digging vintage instruments out, and fixing them, and making them available." Anyone who admired the old instruments "got to know about GTR even if you were a thousand miles away. You got to know that there were these guys down in Nashville that were making some of these instruments available."

In addition to his work on the store's inventory, Randy also performed "outside" repair work: repairs for customers' instruments. With the variety of instruments Randy encountered, he developed novel repair methods for common problems. He was an early adopter of the process to reset guitar necks.

Most early guitar necks were joined to the body at the neck block, where a dovetail joint was reinforced with glue to make a secure connection. Over time, the tension of the guitar strings can cause the entire system of neck, dovetail joint, body, and bridge to distort, which raises the action of the strings over the frets, especially the frets for high notes. The result is a guitar that is difficult to play because of the force required to note a string. In the early 1970s, luthiers commonly solved this problem by filing away material near the nut of the guitar, but this process thinned the neck and affected playability. Even the big guitar manufacturers did not think the problem required disassembling the guitar. According to Gruhn, "Martin believed dovetail joints didn't move."

Randy's technique to solve this problem was to cut the fretboard at the fourteenth fret, expose the underlying dovetail joint, and then introduce hot water to melt the glue. He could then slide the neck off and recontour the dovetail joint so that, when reinstalled, the neck will properly align with the body and strings. It is an efficient method for removing the neck without breaking any wood grains. But the technique is risky, as Randy discovered with one particular repair job that crossed his bench at GTR.

Guitarist Merle Travis once brought his workhorse Gibson Super 400 to Randy because it was becoming difficult to play. "Hell, the action was half inch high, at least," Randy says with exaggeration. "I told him we can reset the neck. I had been resetting necks for all of maybe two years, but I didn't stop to think about what the guitar was. If it needed something done, I'd jump on it and try to do it. I was an idiot back then, I guess." Randy proceeded to apply his neck reset method without hesitation. "I didn't think anything about the neck having been out of it before, because most instruments you'd run into back then, the necks had never been out of them. Nobody was resetting necks back then but me."

He heated the neck block on Travis's guitar longer than usual, because he had trouble loosening the joint. He finally removed the neck late in the day, so he put the project aside to resume the following morning. When he returned to the shop that next day, he was in for a shock. "I came back in the next morning and looked at it, and then I picked the body up, and I happened to turn it around and look at the back, and the back of that damn thing looked like a washboard!" Randy immediately noticed the neck he had removed was not original to the guitar, and for some un-known reason, the new neck he had just removed had a small hole drilled through the neck block, from the dovetail cavity to the guitar body. While Randy was struggling to remove the neck the previous day, steam and water, which would have normally been contained in the cavity, were pouring into the guitar body and soaking the back piece. "I was sick!" Randy says, describing his dread. "I almost had a heart attack. I said, 'What am I gonna do?'"

He thought he might be able to reverse the rippling effect on the back by drying it. So, with a hair dryer and a lot of patience, he spent the morn-ing drying and smoothing out the back. "I finally got it all back, and it came out beautifully," he says. "You couldn't tell anything had happened to it." He finished resetting the neck and then called Travis to retrieve his repaired guitar. Randy explains, "He came by, and he got it and played on it a little while and, boy, he was tickled to death, it played so great. He said it had never played that good when he first got it." Randy was relieved by Travis's reaction, but to clear his conscience, he needed to confess the truth about what took place with the guitar. "I was scared to death; that was his main guitar. But I told him, and he said, 'Ah, don't worry about it. Hell, they got more guitars.' That was all he ever said about it." That Super 400 now resides in the Country Music Hall of Fame.

Fellow Luthiers at GTR

As more repair work filled the workshop, Randy found himself in need of help to keep up. George employed other luthiers to work in the shop to help with the backlog. Anyone who decides to drop everything and build guitars for a living is already swimming against the mainstream, and many of Randy's coworkers were quite colorful. One of the first was a man named Bernie Michelle, who bought Randy's first mandolin. Michelle was a night owl who "would come in as we were getting ready to close," Randy remembers, "and George would lock him in the store. The next morning when we came in to open up, he would be ready to go home." The schedule may have been unconventional, but Randy did not mind. "Bernie was kind of an anti-people person anyway." Randy had also chosen this unconventional career path, but at twenty-six years old—Randy's age at the time of GTR's opening—he already exhibited an ease with his work that other builders admired.

Wayne Henderson, the celebrated guitar builder from Rugby, Virginia, and subject of the book *Clapton's Guitar* by Allen St. John, worked with Randy after Gruhn enticed him to come help with the backlog of repair work. "George would call me every once in a while and want to know if I'd come work, because he'd get behind on repair work," Henderson explains. He was reluctant to leave his rural Virginia home, but George's persistence finally got him to travel to Nashville. Once he decided to go, Henderson was eager to work with Randy at GTR. "I had no doubt heard of him cause he's always been a pretty well-known inlay person and instrument repair guy and everything. But I met him, and he turned out to be really a nice guy, helpful fella, and I was just always really impressed with his work," Henderson says.

Henderson was prepared to meet a great builder, but he did not expect to meet such a pragmatist, too. Randy's no-nonsense ways of getting a job done made an impression on him from day one. The practices were not confined to guitar repair. Henderson recounts:

> When I first met him—one of the strangest things, something I still remember—he would work in that shop, and he drank coffee all the time. He had an old soldering gun that had a big chunk of copper or brass on the end of it, a pointy-shaped thing. It had an electric cord to it. And I think it had sorta gotten shot to where it didn't get hot enough to melt solder and work really good. And he would clamp that thing on the upper shelf and let it dangle down over the work table, and the end of it would hang in his coffee. And it kept his coffee hot all the time. But that thing looked corroded and nasty, and, of course, I guess it had more coffee on it than anything else. But, man alive, I thought, *man he's going to poison himself!* That same old soldering iron hung there all the time. But Randy was the one that had hot coffee all the time.

Henderson was already a competent builder and repairman in his own right, but Randy taught him that confidence, pragmatism, and a hint of swagger are necessary traits of a successful luthier. Henderson remembers a particularly vivid lesson on all three traits. After spending hours trying to remove the top from the front block of the neck of a prewar D-45, which according to Henderson was "the most valuable instrument you could mess with," he finally had to ask for help.

"Randy, have you got any kind of trick to get the top off of this thing?" Henderson asked.

"You've got it loose everywhere except that block, ain't you?" Randy responded.

"Yeah, it's loose everywhere except that," Henderson said, referring to the neck block.

According to Henderson, "Randy reached in there, right in the sound hole, and got a hold of that top and gave one big yank, and BANG, that whole thing come off. I liked to fainted because I thought surely it would bust the whole end out of that top if you did something like that. But bracing was still on it and he said, 'There you go. That's the way to get it off.'" Henderson was stunned. "I didn't know what to think of it. It wasn't his project. If he busted the end off of it, I'd have to fix it. But that really helped. In a second, he had that top off." Looking back, Henderson realizes, "That may have been the safest way to do it. You know, if you keep heating, and picking, and messing, you probably would have gotten that wood hot and probably been more apt to mess it up than just yanking it off there. He seemed to know that's what would happen. He always knows how to get something done" (St. John 2005).

The GTR Bloom Fades

GTR was the realization of a dream for Gruhn, Taylor, and Wood, but keeping the new shop in the black was a struggle. "It was pure magic to have Norman Blake there in our little office/studio and to be able to go back and forth from our shop and the backstage area of the Johnny Cash TV show and meet world-class musicians," Gruhn says, "but I also recall that there were some days when we took in as little as $5 for the entire day's proceeds. We didn't enter the business with delusions of grandeur. It was evident from the start that we were not going to become millionaires overnight in a little 20' × 60' building with only the first 15' devoted to the showroom."

The financial struggles especially strained Tut, who had a large family to support. Tut recalls reaching a point at which, "I decided then maybe I just better not be in the business anymore." In September 1970, George arrived at work one morning and found an envelope taped to the door. According to George, "It said 'George' and it had a hand ball-point pen drawing of a rattlesnake." The letter, written by Tut, read, "George, I have decided that it's just not working anymore for me. I would like to sell my share in the business to you. Call your father and get ten thousand dollars. We'll work out the rest." George was incredulous that Tut assumed George could simply call home and ask for that kind of money. "I couldn't call my Daddy and get ten thousand dollars!" he exclaims. But any bitterness between Tut and George subsided with time. "We worked out a deal, and quite honestly, I don't remember what the deal was anymore, but Tut got some instruments and a little bit of money, and he was gone." George continued to run the shop under the GTR name until 1976, when he changed the name to Gruhn Guitars, Inc. In the following years, Gruhn created one of the most respected vintage instrument stores in the world. Today it is a mecca for musicians along the entire spectrum of ability. It all began when George, Tut, and Randy decided to act on a dream.

Randy remained as the shop repairman until 1972. He maintained his friendship with Tut. But he began to reevaluate his own desire to stay. His restlessness was stoked when Tut began sharing ideas about opening another shop. Always keenly aware of how to pull the right strings to entice his friends, Tut floated the idea that he and Randy could partner for this new venture. Randy was excited about the idea of a new adventure. It would fend off the risk of falling into a dreaded rut. "Tut got to talk about wanting to open up another place. And another friend of ours, Grant Boatwright, kept talking about wanting to do something. He was into instruments, too."

The stage was set for the next chapter in Randy's life. At GTR, he established himself as one of the first and preeminent repairmen in the emerging business of vintage instrument trading. But Randy spent most of his time tucked away in the shop. With Tut's nudging, Randy would soon establish himself at the helm of what was to become an iconic Nashville institution.

Darryl Wolfe and Randy Wood. Photo courtesy of Bobby Wolfe.

Randy Wood. Photo courtesy of Randy Wood.

Randy Wood's Mandolin #1. Photo by Dan Loftin.

Detail of Randy Wood's
Mandolin #1 headstock.
Photo by Dan Loftin.

photo: Mickey Dobo

Mickey Dobo

Randy Wood's Mandolin #2.
Photo by Mickey Dobo.

Detail of Randy Wood's
Mandolin #2 headstock.
Photo by Mickey Dobo.

Randy Wood's Mandolin #3. Photo by Dan Loftin.

Detail of Randy Wood's
Mandolin #3 headstock.
Photo by Dan Loftin.

Tut Taylor, Johnny Cash, and Randy Wood.
Photo courtesy of Randy Wood.

Johnny Cash's acknowledgment to Randy.
Photo courtesy of Randy Wood.

Bobby Whitlock's guitar with Randy Wood inlay.
Photo courtesy of Bobby Whitlock.

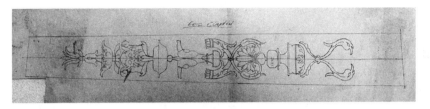

Eric Clapton Dobro inlay pattern sketch.
Photo by Daniel Wile.

Eric Clapton with Dobro showing Randy Wood inlay.
Photo by Larry Hulst via Getty Images.

Elvis Presley inlay pattern sketch. Photo by Daniel Wile.

Elvis Presley's Gibson Dove. ©2019 GracelandAuctions.com.

Randy's inlay on Elvis's Gibson Dove fingerboard.
©2019 GracelandAuctions.com.

Detail of Elvis inlay. ©2019 GracelandAuctions.com.

The music store area in the Old Time Picking Parlor.
Photo by J. D. Sloan.

Randy, heading up "the hippest spot in town,"
according to apprentice Chris Camp.
Photo by J. D. Sloan.

Old Time Picking Parlor jam session. *Left to right:* Bill Keith, Larry Sledge, Frazier Moss, J. T. Gray (on bass), and Jim Johnson (on guitar).
Photo by J. D. Sloan.

The upstairs workshop at the Old Time Picking Parlor.
Photo courtesy of Danny Ferrington.

Randy taking a smoke break in the Old Time Picking Parlor workshop.
Photo courtesy of Danny Ferrington.

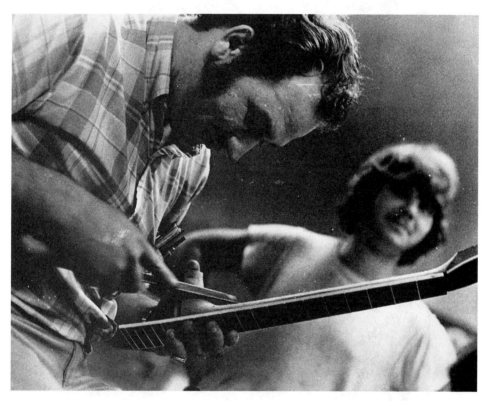
Randy filing a guitar neck.
Photo courtesy of Randy Wood.

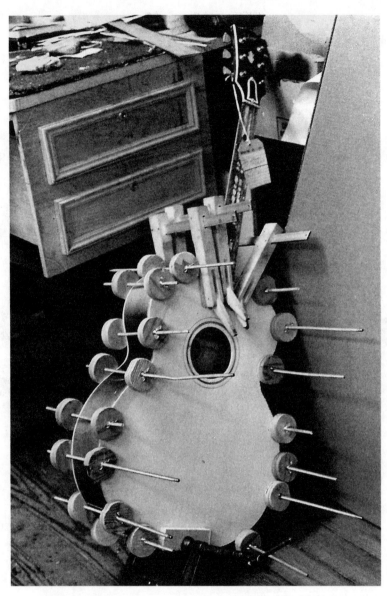

Guitar under construction, clamped while glue dries.
Photo by J. D. Sloan.

Randy inspecting a guitar.
Photo courtesy of Randy Wood.

Apprentice Coley Coleman
learning the tricks of the
trade from Randy.
Photo by J. D. Sloan.

Charlie Collins and Norman Blake share a laugh while jamming.
Photo by J. D. Sloan.

Opry legends "Bashful Brother Oswald" Kirby, Charlie Collins,
and Roy Acuff pose in the Picking Parlor.
Photo by J. D. Sloan.

Charlie Collins and "Bashful Brother Oswald" Kirby jam by
the Picking Parlor's rustic pot-bellied stove.
Photo by J. D. Sloan.

Vassar Clements noodles on the fiddle
while Roland White's son Lawrence Lee looks on.
Photo by J. D. Sloan.

The Whites perform at the Picking Parlor with Norman Blake, Jack Hicks,
Terry Dearborn, and Mark O'Connor. Note the backdrop painted by Tut Taylor.
Photo by J. D. Sloan.

Hatch show print for Whites concert.
Courtesy of Randy Wood.

Informal jamming in the Picking Parlor.
Photo by J. D. Sloan.

Country Gazette (Alan Munde, Dave Ferguson [?], Roger Bush, and Roland White).
Photo by J. D. Sloan.

Country Gazette goofing around on stage.
Photo by J. D. Sloan.

Danny Ferrington and Billy Gibbons of ZZ Top at the Old Time Picking Parlor.
Photo courtesy of Danny Ferrington.

Danny Ferrington at his Picking Parlor workbench.
Photo courtesy of Danny Ferrington.

Apprentices Jerry Jones and Danny Ferrington.
Photo courtesy of Danny Ferrington.

Nancy and Norman Blake sit in for a jam at the Picking Parlor.
Photo courtesy of Danny Ferrington.

Charlie Collins, Mike Pearson, and Bill Monroe perform at the Picking Parlor.
Photo by J. D. Sloan.

Country Gazette in the cavernous Picking Parlor music club, after renovation.
Photo by Dan Loftin.

Bluegrass gives way to edgier sounds at the Picking Parlor after renovation.
Pictured are the Linda Hargrove Band and Willie Nelson.
Photo courtesy of Randy Wood.

The Picking Parlor location in 2011.
Photo by Daniel Wile.

Randy at his Isle of Hope shop.
Photo courtesy of Randy Wood.

Randy on Isle of Hope, Georgia.
Photography by Jake Jacobson.

Sailboat cockpit table built by Randy.
Photo by Daniel Wile.

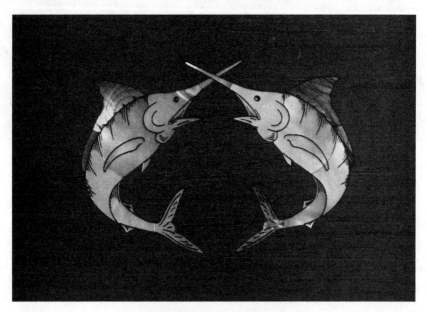

Marlin inlay on sailboat cockpit table.
Photo by Daniel Wile.

The controversial sign at Randy Wood Guitars in Bloomingdale.
Photo by Daniel Wile.

Michael Cleveland and Flamekeeper perform at Randy Wood Guitars.
Photo courtesy of Dennis Satterlee.

Randy contemplating his glue work.
Photo by Daniel Wile.

A Randy Wood mandolin once owned by Clarence White.
Photo by Geoff Winningham.

Randy Wood Guitar. Photo by Richard Leo Johnson.

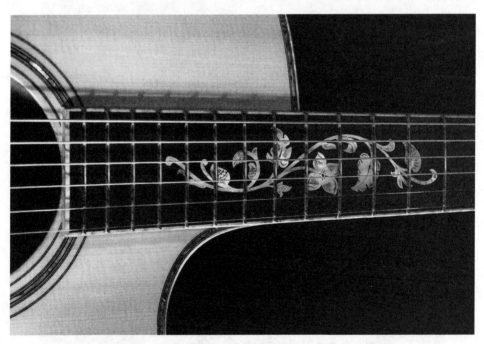

Close-up of the fingerboard inlay. Photo by Richard Leo Johnson.

Randy Wood hollow-body guitar.
Photo by Richard Leo Johnson.

Randy Wood parlor guitar.
Photo by Richard Leo Johnson.

Randy Wood satin wood mandolin. Photo by Daniel Wile.

(*Above*) Detail of satin wood mandolin.
Photo by Daniel Wile.

(*Right*) Hummingbird inlay on satin wood mandolin
fingerboard. Photo by Daniel Wile.

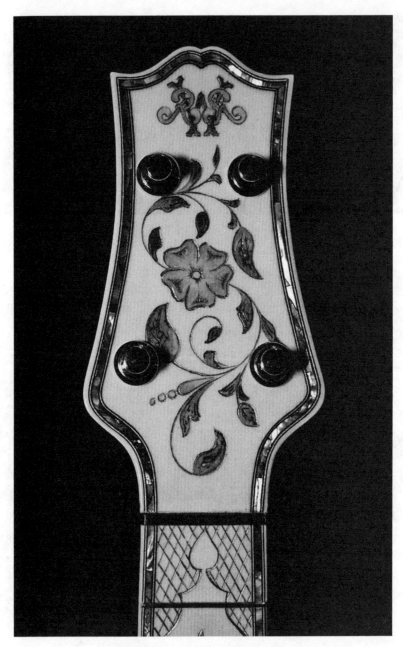

Randy Wood ukulele headstock.
Photo by Mike Davis.

Close-up of the Randy Wood "Phoenix" hollowbody guitar.
Photo by Daniel Wile.

Randy Wood headstock detail.
Photo by Daniel Wile.

Typical workbench in Randy's shop.
Photo by Daniel Wile.

Randy playing with Dick Smith and Eddie Hoover in his Bloomingdale workshop.
Photo by Daniel Wile.

Peter Rowan and Randy Wood in Bloomingdale. Photo by Dennis Satterlee.

Earl Scruggs and Randy Wood in Bloomingdale. Photo by Dennis Satterlee.

Randy and Adam Steffey in Bloomingdale. Steffey is playing
a Randy Wood mandocello. Photo by Dennis Satterlee.

6

THE EARLY DAYS OF THE
PICKING PARLOR

I was just trying to make a living. I didn't even know enough
about business to know I was in business! I just knew I was five
thousand dollars in the hole, and I had a guitar shop.

RANDY WOOD

Another Dream, Another Store

In any discussion about his younger days, Randy is likely to lament, "I didn't have no money." That refrain peppers the stories of his life. So it is remarkable how confidently he jumped from one endeavor to the next, like a trapeze artist letting go of one bar before securely grasping the next. Having "no money" meant having no safety net. In the spring of 1972, as the twenty-seven-year-old Wood parted ways with George Gruhn, he and Tut Taylor shared a dream of opening another music shop of their own. Randy and Tut knew the struggles inherent in opening a music store; GTR had just celebrated only its second anniversary. Yet they wanted another attempt. Their brainchild nearly died in infancy.

The GTR threesome faced long odds from the beginning. The nascent vintage instrument market guaranteed no participants a substantial living. In the fall of 1970, it was bachelor George's low personal overhead that allowed him to survive as the remaining owner after Tut tapped out to find a more dependable income to support his wife and two—out of seven—children still living at home. While Randy stayed with George longer than Tut did, he found limitations in his role at GTR. Randy's job was to repair incoming instruments so they could be justifiably tagged with prices above acquisition and repair costs, thus allowing GTR to earn a profit on the sale. But Randy longed for more. He still harbored a desire to own a music club, just as he had owned the Beachcomber in Brunswick. The job of a backroom technician was not fulfilling, and he left GTR in early 1972. "I think George was almost probably kind of glad to get rid of us," Randy admits. "I stayed there long enough to get John Grevin as a replacement repairman. He moved up there from Chattanooga. I helped get him situated before I left so George had somebody to do repair work."

Randy and Tut talked with each other regularly and shared their dreams of Nashville glory. As the trickle of discussions about another music store turned into a steady flow, Tut and Randy included a mutual friend, Grant Boatwright, in the discussions. Boatwright was a banjo player in a touring bluegrass band, Red White and Bluegrass. "I don't remember who brought up the idea of opening another place," Randy says in retrospect. "I don't know if any of the three of us knows. You know, it was just something that probably came up in conversation, and then the idea took shape." He adds, "We knew we wanted to start a store like a vintage instrument store, like George, because Tut and I both were doing vintage. Grant Boatwright was, too."

The Country Music Scene in the Early 1970s

Meanwhile, the commercial success of country music continued to grow, and women were sharing the prosperity. While Conway Twitty saw huge success with his country hits "Image of Me," "Next in Line," and "Hello Darlin'," his frequent duet partner Loretta Lynn established her own brand after the release of her best-selling autobiography, *Coal Miner's Daughter*. In 1972 she became the first woman to be named the Country Music Association's "Entertainer of the Year." Dolly Parton also emerged from the shadow of Porter Wagoner with her first big hit, "Joshua."

The music evolved as its twangy, honky-tonk sounds gave way to the smoother "Nashville Sound." There were external influences, too, as artists from the rock and folk genres experimented with country music. Many of these musicians did not have a country pedigree—southern, rural, agrarian upbringing—but were nonetheless influenced by the popularity of country and bluegrass music from earlier decades. Bob Dylan recorded *Nashville Skyline* in 1969 with some of the top session musicians in Nashville. Californians John McEuen and Jerry Garcia introduced banjos into the songs of the Nitty Gritty Dirt Band and the Grateful Dead, respectively. The popular singer Linda Ronstadt, raised in Arizona, had a great respect for country music, claiming in a 1970 interview, "Country music is very real and very groovy, and it's exerting so much influence on pop that even the Beatles' 'Revolution' had a country sound to it" (Country Western Stars 1970).

The shift in country created an opportunity for folk and bluegrass to provide a sense of authenticity some traditional country fans missed in the new songs being recorded in Nashville. These fans flocked to folk and bluegrass. However, as folk and bluegrass gained popularity, younger audiences discovered the genres and interpreted them with modern perspectives. New Grass Revival, one of the most progressive bluegrass bands of any era took shape in the early 1970s. New Grass Revival mandolinist Sam Bush exemplified the group's character, with his "enthusiasm, his wild and extended improvisations, his perfectionism, and his tireless experimentations with other forms of music" (Malone 2010, 363).

The dynamic environment made Nashville a melting pot for musicians from many genres. As the lines between musical styles blurred and the formulas for success changed, one thing remained true of the music being made in the 1970s: musicians still needed acoustic instruments, and they still needed someone to repair them when they were damaged.

Finding a Home

Tut and Randy began looking for a building where they could bring to life the idea of a new store. Grant Boatwright's busy tour schedule kept him out of the building search process. Tut located a building at 105 Second Avenue, just a couple of blocks away from GTR, facing the Cumberland riverfront. While GTR took form in a rented building, Tut recommended buying property at the low prices available in the market at the time, as downtown real estate had hardly grown any more desirable in the year and a half since the search for GTR's storefront. "We started looking for a place and found a building down there, actually it was two buildings, for sale," Randy says of the real estate search. They thought the price was attractive, but they would soon learn that they missed, by a matter of days, an opportunity to practically steal the property. "We missed buying it on the courthouse steps by like two weeks," Randy says with regret. He remembered paying twenty thousand dollars for the downtown building. "It was a good price back then, but it wasn't *that* good a price. The guy that we got it from had bought it two weeks before on the courthouse steps." Despite missing out on an auction bargain, Randy confesses that it was, nonetheless, "a pretty good deal for us."

Suddenly Randy, Tut, and Grant Boatwright found themselves in possession of two adjoining buildings on a seedy section of Second Avenue in Nashville. They planned to open a music store on the first floor of one building and a repair shop on the second floor. Explaining their plans, Randy says, "One whole building we were using just for storage. When we bought it, we had to buy both buildings, but we only needed, at the time, the one building."

Tut and Randy proceeded to claim their spaces in the building for their roles in the business. They allocated the front half of the downstairs to be the music store. With knotty pine paneling, "it made a real nice music store," according to Randy. Tut created a small sign-painting shop in the back half of the ground floor. Randy says, "Tut was going to make money making signs on the side. His main job with the corporation was to run the retail part of the store. He was downstairs and he'd be painting a sign, and if he heard somebody come in, he could go out there and wait on them." Randy would primarily spend his time upstairs in the repair shop.

The starting capital was meager, but the three put up what little they had to get the fledgling store up and running. "We each put up the equivalent of five thousand dollars," Randy explains. "That could consist of cash money, or instruments, or parts, or machinery, whatever. Tut and Grant both put up a good many instruments, plus some cash money, and I put up some cash money plus woodworking equipment and one or two extras, but mostly woodworking equipment." Randy owned some of his tools at

GTR, and he took "patterns and jigs and stuff like that" he had accumulated. "Tut and Grant both had, I think, over a dozen instruments apiece. All of it was nice stuff back then."

Opening a new music store was gutsy, especially since the challenges of a fledgling business were fresh in their minds. But Randy remained optimistic, showing the same confidence his father validated in the Brunswick hobby shop, the same confidence Wayne Henderson observed in Randy's bold repair techniques. Looking back on the early days of the venture with Tut and Grant, Randy says, "I was just trying to make a living. I didn't even know enough about business to know I was in business! I just knew I was five thousand dollars in the hole, and I had a guitar shop."

The Old Time Picking Parlor Is Born

The three men chose a curious name for a retail store: The Old Time Picking Parlor. Randy maintains that their aim was to open a music shop that would sell and repair instruments. However, the chosen name insinuated this shop would be more than just a place to buy and sell. It was meant to be a place for hanging out and playing music. Whether or not the partners had this in mind when they named the enterprise, the little store would soon live up to its name.

Incidentally, the actual name of the business conformed to proper spelling, despite popular opinion. Business cards and photographs of the storefront sign confirm that "Old Time Picking Parlor" was the name. However, countless newspaper and magazine articles have mistakenly referred to it as the "Old Time Pickin' Parlor." Perhaps the laidback, mostly rural background of the store owners and patrons made the shortened "Pickin'" seem fitting. Or perhaps the fact that Randy has never enunciated the ending "g" misled interviewers who did not actually see the store's name in print. Regardless, grammarians can rest assured that the "g" was not dropped in the official name—in print, at least.

The Old Time Picking Parlor opened for business in July 1972. Randy was one month shy of his twenty-ninth birthday. In contrast to GTR's opening two and a half years earlier, Randy and Tut enjoyed more name recognition this time, thanks to a growing network of Nashville friends and patrons.

Sam Bush and "Hoss"

An early customer of the Picking Parlor was mandolinist Sam Bush. Randy had met him when Bush was still a teenager making the rounds of the bluegrass festival circuit. For a few years Bush even played one of Randy's A-model mandolin conversions. Not long after the Picking Parlor opened, Norman Blake brought a 1937 Gibson F-5 mandolin to Randy for much-needed care. As Randy colorfully describes, "It looked like it had been drug behind a car for a while, and a herd of hogs ran over it." Bush had a chance to play the instrument before it went under Randy's care, and Randy says Bush did not like the sound. "The mandolin looked so bad and it sounded so bad that Tut and I decided to refinish it," Randy says. "Since we were going to refinish it, we decided to take it apart and regraduate it and redo the tone bars. And I think maybe we reset the neck. We did a major overhaul on the thing. We completely stripped it. It didn't have much finish on it anyway. We basically just sanded everything down pretty smooth and put a finish back on it." The refurbished mandolin was completely reborn. Bush again came by the store, and Randy says, "He picked it up and played on it a little while and fell in love with it." During an interview with Ari Surdoval, Sam Bush told of his amazement of the mandolin's transformation, saying, "The next time I heard the mandolin I couldn't believe it. I couldn't believe it was the same instrument." Norman Blake traded the mandolin to Tut, but soon afterward, Bush pleaded with Tut for it and eventually persuaded Tut to part with the mandolin. Since then, it has served as his primary mandolin—his workhorse—throughout his storied career. He affectionately calls it "Hoss."

The Old Time Picking Parlor Develops Its Character

Business trickled into the Old Time Picking Parlor, but Randy, Tut, and Grant avoided the temptation to coerce visitors into spending money. That may have been questionable for a young, vulnerable business, but it allowed visitors to relax. When Randy ran the Beachcomber in Brunswick, he encouraged his friends to hang out and play music. Now that he was part-owner of the Picking Parlor and not confined to the back, as he was at GTR, he felt free to encourage the activity. He liked having musicians around, and he also observed that "people kept coming in wanting to jam. There was really no good place to jam." The cavernous space he and Tut had just purchased offered a solution. "We had the other building next door, [and] there was a big door into the other building. So we put some chairs in there, and when some pickers came around wanting to jam, we'd all go in there and pick. That got to be a regular thing." Soon the ad hoc music became an attraction to visitors. "People would start bringing their friends. So people started coming by to listen." Visitors were beginning to spend enough time in the Picking Parlor that they felt comfortable enough to ask for refreshments. Randy was happy to oblige. "We set up a little old coffee pot in there so we'd have some coffee, and I think we even bought a few soft drinks." Randy and Tut later added a stage to the picking room to create a space more conducive to performances. Before Randy, Tut, and Grant realized what had happened, they found themselves running a music club in addition to the main store and repair shop.

The club became a big attraction for the Picking Parlor, with live music Tuesday through Saturday. After a full day in the workshop and music store, Randy—with Irene's help—kept the night club open until midnight most weeknights and until two in the morning on Friday and Saturday nights. They eventually served alcohol and food, as well. Explaining the rationale for having food, Randy says, "Back in those days in Tennessee, you had to derive more than fifty percent of your sales from food in order to have a liquor license. Nobody did that, but I think you had to have at least two items on your menu." The Picking Parlor's menu included frozen pizza and one of Randy's favorite dishes, great northern beans. "Irene would cook up a big pot of great northern beans and we would do these cornbread fritters. We'd serve a bowl of beans, a couple of fritters, and a slice of onion. We sold a lot of that stuff," Randy boasts.

With the vacant building now housing activity, Tut Taylor was struck by an idea to exploit his painting talent to personalize the new picking room. He decided to decorate the walls with enormous murals. "I painted a huge D-45, and right in the center of the stage was the sound hole. If you sat in a chair, your head would come about to the top of the sound hole. Then I painted a big set of fingerpicks, thumb and two fingerpicks on the wall, and might have been an F-5 mandolin," Tut recalls. Doug Green, in a *Pickin'* article about the Picking Parlor, described the murals which "[dominated] the room. . . . On the far wall (facing the stage) is an informal sketch—that is nearly life size—of John Hartford, Norman Blake, Tut, and Vassar Clements on stage," the foursome commonly known as the Steam Powered Aereo-Plain Band. "To the left of the stage is a monstrous color rendition of a Dobro, and right behind the stage, the huge, beautifully colored body of a Martin D-45." Green was impressed, gushing that Tut had "obviously mastered his craft; his contribution to the Pickin' Parlor is easily one of its most distinctive attractions, and certainly adds both warmth and humor" to the otherwise empty adjacent building (Green 1976). Referring to the Picking Parlor with its lively music room next to the shop, Tut says, "A lot of hanging out and pickin' went on there. It was just the 'in' place to be. Oswald [Kirby] would come by a lot. [Roy] Acuff came down all the time" (Johnson 2011).

A Rift with Tut

They may have had a good thing going for visitors, but the business struggled to stay afloat. According to Randy, instruments were coming into the store and going straight into Tut's personal collection. Randy helplessly observed this because he lacked the cash to compete with Tut's offers. One day Tut laid bare the facts to Randy. "He told me, 'We're in bankruptcy. It's just a matter of us filing papers. We ain't got no money; we ain't got no assets. Most of the instruments belong to me personally.'" This was news to Randy, as he assumed "these were instruments I thought we had bought." He quickly discovered his naivety. "Unbeknownst to me, Tut had bought them with his money rather than the store's money. But in the meantime, he was paying the bills, and everything else, with the store's money." The Old Time Picking Parlor was bleeding money, and because Grant Boatwright was on the road with his band and absent from much of this period in the store's life, Randy had to confront his circumstance without a supporting partner.

Randy suspected Tut had found an angle in the Picking Parlor's financial straits. He presumed Tut ultimately wanted sole ownership of the building, a sizable piece of Nashville real estate. "We had put a clause in the contract at Tut's insistence," Randy explains, "that if one partner wanted to buy the other partners out, he would make those two partners an offer. If either of the other two partners wanted to counter that offer, they could counter that offer. If he wasn't willing to match that offer, whoever made the highest offer could buy the other two out, even if they didn't want to sell out." Randy suspected that Tut hoped to buy out the two other partners at a cheap price and own the building outright. "He knew that I didn't have any money, so I couldn't buy the place, and he knew Grant didn't have any money, of course. Grant had to borrow the money to buy in to begin with. So he just said, 'We're basically bankrupt. I'm going to go ahead and file bankruptcy papers, and then I'll buy the building back from the bankruptcy court.'" Randy, incredulous, asked what he and Grant were supposed to do now that they faced losing their stake in the business. Tut replied, "I'll hire you to continue to work here, and I'll pay you two thousand dollars for your third interest." Randy says, "I didn't really have any choice in the matter, I thought."

Randy may have felt he was out of options, but he was not yet ready to surrender. He was not willing to see his dream of being a Nashville music store owner crumble before it had fully cured. There was, however, one trump card left in his hand; he just needed help realizing how to play it. "A friend of mine found out about the impending bankruptcy. He was a pretty regular customer, and he came by my house and asked me if what was going on was true, if we were going to go bankrupt. I didn't know nothing about business, but if Tut says we ain't got no money, I guess we don't." The man asked Randy if he wanted to run the business or let Tut take it over. Randy wanted to run the Picking Parlor, since he did not like his alternatives. He felt he did not "have anywhere to go, except maybe to move back to Muscle Shoals, or go back and work for George, or go to work for Sho-Bud." The friend told Randy about a local banker who might be able to help and suggested that Randy visit him and mention the referral. Randy visited the bank and explained his predicament.

"How much money do you need?" the banker asked.

"Well, Tut's offered me $2,000, so I'm probably going to have to offer him $2,200 or something, to buy him out. And I want to pay Grant the same thing. I don't feel like leaving Grant in the cold."

"If you give them $2,250 a piece, that'd be $4,500. Why don't I make out the loan for $6,000? That'll give you money to buy them out and to get stuff transferred over—licenses and stuff like that."

Randy was speechless. He accepted the bank's offer, hardly pausing to think about the commitment he was making. "Hell, I wasn't thinking," Randy confesses in retrospect. "He gave me a $6,000 signature loan. He'd never met me before. Just did it on that friend of mine's say-so."

Six thousand dollars improved Randy's negotiating position immensely. He promptly went back to Tut not only to halt the bankruptcy filing but to turn the tables and make a buyout offer. When Randy broke the news, "Tut went through the roof. He was pissed." Randy explained to Tut there was no choice except for him to sell, but Tut vowed to fight it. "Well, it was his attorney that had drawn up the papers," Randy says, acknowledging the irony of Tut's anger. "So I called the guy. I didn't know him very well, but I explained the situation to him, and he said, 'I'm sorry, but if Tut doesn't better that offer, he'll have to sell.'" Randy explained that Tut had made it clear he would not sign any papers or accept any amount of money. The attorney offered to sign the papers and hold the money in escrow if Tut remained obstinate. Tut did, and Randy inked the deal with the attorney. Tut did not even attend the closing. "I didn't know it at the time, but Tut went down to the Picking Parlor that morning, while we were at the lawyer's office, and he took all his instruments out." It was a sudden end of a partnership that had seemed so promising only a few months prior.

The parting was bitter, but Tut and Randy respected each other too much to allow the feud over the business to last long. "We had some problems at the time," Randy says, "but as far as I was concerned, he pretty well got over them. It all turned out okay for me, so I didn't have any animosity toward Tut. I had learned a lot from Tut. Tut was instrumental in me getting into this business." Tut was too experienced with the vagaries of deal-making to let his emotions keep him down for long. Late in his life Tut chose to remember the excitement he felt in those early days of the Picking Parlor. He told interviewer Orville Johnson (2011), "Oh, we had a good thing and didn't know it, man."

Randy hoped he had a good thing, but when he assessed his situation, it appeared bleak. "I had a music store with a little ol' junky cash register, and had a few sets of strings, and a few picks, very few little odds and ends, and two metal body Dobros. And back then, you couldn't give a metal body Dobro away to nobody. They would almost pay you to take them. That's what I had for store stock." Randy found himself as the sole owner of the Old Time Picking Parlor, a music store with only two instruments to its name. Until that point, Randy had never thought of himself as a business owner. He says he thought of himself as "working for a company. I was more of an employee." That all changed when he bought out Tut and Grant. The Picking Parlor had a lot of empty space after their departure. But that space became room to grow. For nearly three years, Randy had been the guy in the back shop. Finally there was room for not only the luthier but also for the nightclub owner and the benevolent host who welcomed talented musicians of all stripes because he loved their company. Randy finally had the place where the outlets for his passions could flourish with a synergy that would make the Old Time Picking Parlor legendary.

PICKING PARLOR IN FULL SWING

*It was a magic time, and Randy was
heading up the hippest spot in town.*

———————

CHRIS CAMP

In the February 1976 issue of *Pickin'* magazine, "Ranger" Doug Green guides readers on a tour of the Old Time Picking Parlor. Green captures the essence of "one of the few must-see attractions in Bluegrass" by recognizing that the Picking Parlor was not just a bluegrass club, a music store, or a repair shop; it was all three. "Therein lies its success and its uniqueness," Green observes. Green provides readers a detailed portrait of "easily one of the most charming and entertaining places in Nashville" at the height of its popularity.

The tour guides readers vicariously through "three separate and unique businesses under one heading and one roof." The first tour stop is the sales area, "a cozy, wood-paneled room, ringed with rows of lovely instruments, many rare, most hard to get. This guitar store segment of the building is not large, but it is comfortable (several chairs surround an old wood stove), and at most any hour of the day a handful of pickers can often be found, rehashing old tunes or learning new ones in as relaxed an atmosphere as can be found." Green further explains that the "laid-back atmosphere encourages friendly visiting and jamming," and "it's not uncommon to see some exceptional musicians sitting around in those chairs jamming for the fun of it. It is occasionally difficult even to enter through the door during peak pickin' times, but there always seems to be room for one more."

The tour continues into the music club, which readers could find "located in a room exceedingly long and narrow, which must be entered through a door in the sales/display room. Although one would expect the acoustics to be unpredictable at best, they are, in fact, rather good, due to an expensive PA system Randy went to some trouble to install, and a series of baffles on the wall which, far from detracting from the appearance of the room, actually give it character. Something of the feel of being in on a recording session is imparted due to the studiolike appearance of the baffling, and they also give a warm, cozy appearance to a room which was too stark without them." Green observes that fans in the club "are usually sophisticated enough not to ask visiting bands for 'Rocky Top.' Yet there is more to it than just this for the visiting musician. Alan Munde of *Country Gazette* sums it up: 'There's just more of a homey-type atmosphere here than at any of the other clubs we play.' It's as true for the audience as it is for him" (Green 1976).

Unfortunately, the tour does not include Randy's upstairs workshop. But it is likely Green would have observed Randy working quietly among several young, quirky apprentices and maybe a few friends who had earned entry into this sanctum that cradled its inhabitants with piles of wood scraps, instrument fragments, tools, jigs, and the aroma of sawdust and nitrocellulose lacquer, all bathed under cool fluorescent light.

In his book *Bluegrass*, Neil Rosenberg recognizes the Picking Parlor as part of a new wave of venues that were making bluegrass music more accessible to a wider audience—an audience that increasingly included urban dwellers who wanted to claim some connection to the rural heritage of the genre:

> The ambience of the Old Time Pickin' Parlor resembled that of other new bluegrass clubs opening in the early seventies. Unlike the rough and tumble bars that had been the primary locale for bluegrass bands in earlier times, these places were consciously, even self-consciously, countrified in décor. Like the Storefront Congregation in Louisville and the Picking Parlor Restaurant in New Haven, Connecticut, Nashville's Pickin' Parlor had gingham tablecloths, potbellied stoves, and other folksy fitting in its décor. It became a meeting place for

local and visiting bluegrass and old-time musicians, and presented at one time or another on its stage virtually every active bluegrass group. (Rosenberg 1985)

Randy had brought a piece of the rural South to Nashville and plugged a hole that opened as country was trending toward pop.

The laidback atmosphere was a reflection of Randy's calm demeanor, even though he had plenty to be stressed about, following the breakup of the partnership with Taylor and Boatwright. He was the sole owner of a struggling, leveraged business whose inventory had been decimated in the fallout of the partnership. Additionally, he was supporting a young family. How did he survive? "I worked my ass off!" he says emphatically. "We opened at ten o'clock, and it was me. I was the only one there. Irene occasionally would come down for a while. . . . We only had one vehicle, and she had Renee." The schedule was demanding for one person. Randy elaborated, "I'd try to get in there about eight or eight-thirty, and I'd work upstairs in the shop doing repair work or whatever until ten, and then I would open up. Then if somebody that I knew came by, I would get them to watch the store for a few minutes while I ran upstairs and did a little job or whatever, any way I could to get work. Otherwise, I was sitting down there all day." He brought his work downstairs as much as possible so he could tend the store while finishing simple tasks, such as restringing guitars. "Then at six o'clock, I would close, go home, eat supper, and come back down there and work until ten-thirty or eleven." It was a grueling schedule that only lasted for the first month of his tenure as sole owner, but Randy says, "It seemed like I did that for a year!"

J. T. Gray

Help arrived in the form of a young, unemployed machinist named J. T. Gray. According to Randy, Gray "would come by and hang out. I'd get him to watch the store while I went and did something." After two or three weeks, Randy told Gray, "If you're gonna be here watching the store all the time, I might as well hire you. I ain't got no money to pay you nothing, but if I ever get some, I'll start paying you." Gray was a natural fit for the

Picking Parlor. He enjoyed the atmosphere there, and he played in a band, the Misty Mountain Boys, that performed often at the Picking Parlor's music club.

J. T. Gray now carries the torch for bluegrass preservation in downtown Nashville as the owner and operator of the Station Inn, a cozy, rustic music club standing its ground in the rapidly gentrifying Gulch district of Nashville. But it was at the Picking Parlor where he found one of his earliest footholds in town:

> I moved to Nashville in 1970. [After a few years] the band I was with started playing down there [at the Picking Parlor] on a regular basis.... Randy needed somebody to help in the store, the counter and everything. I wasn't doing anything but playing some, so I took that job and went to work with him there. It was a great relationship. He had to be one of the best guys to ever work for—just cool. It was hard to get Randy upset on anything. I don't think I ever saw him get irate with a customer. He did what he did, and that was it.

Gray has adopted Randy's managerial style, quietly molding the Station Inn into a welcoming destination for modern enthusiasts of traditional bluegrass music.

The Picking Parlor Scene

With Gray's help, Randy's struggling business gained traction. It did not hurt that Randy's was practically the only vintage repair shop in town. "George Gruhn was there, but he wasn't taking in any outside repairs," Randy claims. "Pretty soon, repair work kept coming in, and I'd build a few. Finally, when we'd get a few bucks, we'd buy another instrument and put it on the wall." In this way, the Picking Parlor's inventory recovered, one instrument at a time.

Once word spread that Randy was open for repairs and had instruments hanging on the wood-paneled walls, musicians flocked to him, just as they had done at GTR and the Picking Parlor before the split with Taylor and Boatwright. For the professional musician, it was a natural place to spend time. Bil VornDick, a preeminent recording engineer and producer, explains, "Think of all the bands that toured. All their instruments had to be repaired. There were only a few in Nashville who could do it, and Randy was it. So when you're sitting around, and Randy would say, 'I can get you a new fret job. Bring it down this afternoon,' that person, instead of driving all the way back home, would sit around and pick with whoever was there." To be sure, there were other bluegrass music clubs, "but nothing where you would jam during the day." For the bluegrass addicts, "It would be an excuse to tell your wife or your girlfriend that you gotta go look at a new capo or you gotta get some strings, and be gone for the rest of the day. . . . It was a great escape." In short, VornDick declares, "That's where everybody hung in Nashville."

Roland White, owner of Randy Wood Mandolin #2, was one of those professionals hanging out there. White recalls, "It was just the best place. . . . Gosh, it was just amazing! When I was in town, I would just go there every Saturday afternoon and jam with people." White, an accomplished player in his own right, was awed by the musicians he saw at the Picking Parlor. "I saw everybody in the business there."

Randy's place was a prime spot for star-gazing. VornDick remembers that "Tut Taylor would be there. Tony Rice, Sam Bush, John Hartford. The list goes on and on." John Hedgecoth frequently hung out at the Picking Parlor and occasionally played bass in gigs at the music club. "Randy's place was really a focal point," he says. "There was always a jam session going on there. And everyone would come down. Bill Monroe would walk in and play, and all the fiddle players would come down there. It was just a great time to be in Nashville if you were into old-time country music and bluegrass, because it was really coming into its own." Hedgecoth recalls playing bass one night while Vassar Clements and Noboru Marishige—or "Shige," as he was known—traded licks on the Picking Parlor stage. "I've never seen anybody stand toe-to-toe with Vassar Clements, like in a cutting contest, and trade solos, and be able to keep up. Vassar could play through the stratosphere. But Shige could do it. He would better Vassar, every chorus he took. And I got to stand behind him, playing bass at the Old Time Picking Parlor and watch this go on."

The *Circle* Effect

Vassar Clements was just one of many traditional bluegrass musicians whose work gained respect and exposure thanks to the popularity of the Nitty Gritty Dirt Band's 1972 album *Will the Circle Be Unbroken*. The Nitty Gritty Dirt Band had been known as a folk-rock group, but after the success of their cover of "Mr. Bojangles," they returned to the roots of the music on which they were raised. The band released *Circle* as a three-disc album of collaborations with many of their heroes, including Maybelle Carter, Doc Watson, Merle Travis, Roy Acuff, and Vassar Clements. The album release was a watershed event for bluegrass. It reached number four on the Billboard country music album charts. As Pete Finney wrote for the Library of Congress, "The success of 'Circle' catapulted some of the featured artists into revived careers and likely helped spur on the growth of bluegrass festivals and record sales for all kinds of rural 'roots' music."

The timing could not have been better for Randy. The growing popularity of bluegrass and bluegrass festivals heightened the public's appreciation for the acoustic instruments—guitars, mandolins, banjos—featured so prominently in the album. Also, several of the album's featured musicians, such as Clements and Acuff, were Picking Parlor regulars. That only added to the Picking Parlor's reputation as a must-see destination for a Nashville tourist.

Randy's Respect for the Players

While the Picking Parlor is often remembered as a celebrity hangout, Randy resisted capitalizing on the opportunity for gawking. Randy viewed the crowd as his extended family. In his eyes, "everybody pretty much in bluegrass knew everybody." He prided himself on providing an atmosphere that made visitors feel at ease. "The stars felt comfortable there," he says. "They knew that they could come in and not have damn flashbulbs going off in their face every two seconds and autograph hounds bothering them." Did music fans not realize that stars were hanging out at the Picking Parlor? Randy explains, "They did to some extent, but we didn't encourage star-gazing. We wouldn't stop somebody from doing it.

If somebody came in and said, 'Hey, do you think so and so would mind me going over to get his autograph?' I'd say, 'Well, probably not, but they're in there just having a nice quiet drink and would probably rather be left alone.'" Ed Foote explains music was the great equalizer within the walls of the Picking Parlor. "A lot of the famous people, when they were in there, they were playing. Who's going to walk up to Chet Atkins and make him stop playing to sign an autograph? No, they were picking."

John McEuen, multi-instrumentalist of the Nitty Gritty Dirt Band, appreciates Randy's respect for professional musicians' personal space. He was one of those celebrity musicians hanging out at the Picking Parlor. "There were no stars," he explains. "There really aren't. That's all a matter of marketing and advertising. There are people that play, and there are people that play that are successful, and some that aren't. That's the feeling you would get with Randy." He adds, "You could go there and just be." The Nitty Gritty Dirt Band was riding a wave of huge success in the wake of the *Circle* album when McEuen discovered the Picking Parlor. But, he says, "To go in there, I felt like I was twenty years old again, trying to figure out how to play 'Bill Cheatham' or something. And if I were trying to figure out how to play 'Bill Cheatham,' if I hung around long enough, the mandolin player or fiddle player that knew it would be in."

Buck White, the patriarch of the country and bluegrass band The Whites, remembers, "Sometimes you'd have somebody who'd come in from out of town who wanted to go where the music was," so they would find their way to the Picking Parlor. "They might want to get your picture or something, but they didn't worry you with it."

No matter what they are called—stars, celebrities, musicians—there were a lot of them hanging around the Picking Parlor. They were part of the character of the place. "You never knew when somebody famous would walk in," Randy says. "A lot of them liked hanging out there when they were in town. Billy Gibbons [of ZZ Top] was one. If he got in town a day early or something, you'd have to put up with him all day. He'd come out there and just hang out in the shop. He enjoyed instruments and liked the shop and the people in there. He knew he could be relaxed. He didn't have to worry about saying something and reading it in the paper the next day."

Ed Foote remembers stumbling upon his heroes when he walked in the Picking Parlor for the first time. "I walked in," he says, "and Charlie Collins and Norman Blake were sitting around picking, doodling around in front. Anybody that walked in could pick a guitar up off the wall and sit in." On a subsequent visit, "Doc and Merle Watson walked in." Foote was in awe. "Here was Doc sitting around picking, saying, 'This is okay, Merle. Here, let me try another one.' He'd hand it to Merle, and Merle would go and get another one off the wall and say, 'Well, Daddy, here's a '42 D-28.' 'Well, let me try that.' There's five or six of us that are just ga-ga." Foote visited the Picking Parlor frequently, drinking in the thrill of being surrounded by his heroes. "John Hartford liked to hang out down there a lot," Foote remembers about the banjoist and songwriter. "He'd come down there and just hang out for hours, sitting in the back, playing everything that was on the rack. We soaked it up." Randy usually stayed quiet, focused on his work. But he enjoyed the atmosphere, just as his visitors did. "Randy likes to have good music around him," Foote says of Randy. Providing a safe space for top-notch players was a way for Randy to attract them.

J. T. Gray was as mesmerized as the customers were. "The biggest thrill for me, working in the store, was the jam sessions that used to go on there. People like Norman Blake, Vassar Clements, Paul Warren, Charlie Collins . . . just sat out there around the old wood heater we had, and they would jam for hours."

For their part, the music celebrities respected the egalitarianism of the Picking Parlor. Dottie West, the country music singer known as much for her beauty as for her songs, once approached Randy to ask if he would allow the Picking Parlor to be used for a benefit concert to raise money for a cancer-stricken family member of an MCA Records employee. Randy readily agreed. On the morning of the event, Randy claims she showed up at the Picking Parlor front door "in her Levis and button-up shirt, and her hair tied up."

"Where's the cleaning stuff?" she asked. "I'm here to go to work."

"What the hell are you talking about?" Randy responded.

"Well, I know y'all gotta clean things up. I'm here to do my part."

Randy was flabbergasted.

Careers Shaped by Randy and the Picking Parlor

But Randy never intended to create a celebrity zoo for public gazing. He was in business to use his abilities to improve the lives of musicians. As John Hedgecoth observes, "He loves the music, and he loves the people that play. He really wanted to produce instruments that they would want to play." Randy's influence reached far beyond just the instruments he built and repaired. According to Bil VornDick, "There's no telling how many hundreds of musicians he's encouraged and helped find a path or helped them network. There are very few people like that out there." VornDick believes that "many thousands of musicians found their way with the help of Randy, not only musically but career-wise."

Randy remembers helping Don Schlitz before Schlitz went on to song-writing fame by penning such hits as "The Gambler," "Forever and Ever, Amen," and "When You Say Nothing at All." Randy says of Schlitz, "I would use him as an opening act. We paid the opening acts twenty-five dollars." The gesture was not completely altruistic. Randy needed entertainers to fill his music club calendar. But he also enjoyed nurturing fledgling artists by giving them a spot on his stage. Some influential people in the music business were likely to be in attendance. "You never knew who was going to be out in the audience," Randy boasts.

Paul Craft, another songwriter, often tried out his new material on the Picking Parlor stage. Although the Nashville Songwriters Hall of Fame would later induct Craft for songs such as "Dropkick Me, Jesus, through the Goalpost of Life," he wrote some duds he was able to flush, thanks to feedback from Picking Parlor performances. "He had one that Irene chewed him out about," Randy recalls with a chuckle. "He had one he had just written that he tried out on the audience there. It was 'Linda Lovelace, Come Sit on My Face.' That was back when the movie *Deep Throat* was so big. But nobody ever picked that one up and recorded it that I know of."

Before reaching country music stardom, Buck White and his daughters, Cheryl and Sharon, struggled to make ends meet while chasing their dream of playing music professionally. "They had just moved to Nashville when we did," Randy says of the White family. "They were having a tough time of it, but I would use them . . . once a month, maybe more than that, just so they could make money to buy groceries." Country music fans know Buck White as a musician, but he was a plumber by trade. Randy even called on him during a renovation of the Picking Parlor, although Randy was dumbfounded that White still practiced plumbing after seeing success as a musician. White recalls, "He needed some restrooms. I put him some real nice restrooms up front. That's what I did for a living. Randy couldn't figure out why I was fooling with that. He was surprised to know that I was something else besides a picker." White's story reflects the spirit of humility that permeated the Picking Parlor.

A perennial fixture—and exemplar of humility—in the confines of the Picking Parlor was Charlie Collins, the longtime sideman in Roy Acuff's Misty Mountain Boys band. Collins was a lot like Randy, soft-spoken, polite, well-trimmed, which is probably why he felt so at home at the Picking Parlor. Like Randy, Collins had a rural upbringing. Also like Randy, he had a work ethic that would ensure a good living despite the vagaries of the music business. "I was working in a shirt factory in East Tennessee," he recalls. "I was a shipping foreman. I thought I was a good one. I must have been because my boss told me, 'Charlie, if you go to Nashville and don't make it, and I'm still here, your job will be open.' So I couldn't lose." But mostly he resembled Randy's humility and dedication to his craft.

When he was not on the road with Acuff, Collins claims, "I stayed at the Picking Parlor. I met a lot of people there." Why was he drawn to spend so much time there? He responds like many others. "I loved it so much. People were interesting to me that came in there. There were pickers that could play things I wanted to hear and wanted to learn in those days. Norman Blake and Vassar Clements, we'd hang out there and play music and just have a great time. I met some wonderful musicians, some of the greatest." Collins also found a welcoming host. "Randy was so nice to us all. I'm sure there were times he would have liked to have done something or closed the door and went someplace else, but not Randy. He stayed right with us."

Collins's musicianship, along with his reputation as a man of his word, earned the respect of many of Nashville's movers and shakers. A recommendation from him had the heft to launch a career in the Music City.

In fact, launching careers was a de facto duty he shared with Randy. "There were boys that would come in and play that I would recommend to somebody," Collins says. He remembers helping a young banjo player from Ft. Payne, Alabama, named James McKinney. "He and I sat there one Saturday morning," Collins says of McKinney. "I said, 'Man, this kid's good.' And not too long after that, somebody asked me about a banjo player, and I said, 'I know a kid in Ft. Payne, Alabama, that would really suit you.' So he got with James, and it worked for him." Collins's assessment was validated when McKinney won the coveted National Banjo Championship at Winfield, Kansas, in 1982.

Randy and Charlie Collins both had a hand in discovering one of the great modern fiddlers, Mark O'Connor. Collins and fellow Acuff sideman "Bashful Brother Oswald" Kirby were playing in the Picking Parlor music club one night in 1974 when a woman with two children walked in. "I happened to be working the door that night," Randy remembers. "They came in about halfway through the first set—Mark, his sister, and his mama. He asked me if we ever let individuals play on stage." Randy responded, saying he did not mind as long as Collins and Kirby did not. "I told him that they would be taking a break in a few minutes, and if he wanted me to, I'd be glad to ask them. He had his case with him. He was six foot tall, a big ol' boy. But you could tell he was real young." O'Connor was twelve years old at the time.

Randy was welcoming, but he was not naïve. He had seen his share of imposters trying to grab attention by claiming they had stage-worthy talent. "You'd get people who wouldn't know one end of an instrument from the other trying to get up and play with you if you weren't careful," Randy says as though he learned from making that mistake. "So, during a break between sets, Collins and Kirby went back to Randy's office to relax, and Randy told them about a young kid who asked to play on stage.

"Can he play?" Collins asked.

"I don't know if he can play or not. I don't know who he is," Randy replied.

"Maybe we better try him out, see if he can play before we get him on-stage," Collins said.

Randy brought the youngster back to meet Collins and Kirby. Collins suggested O'Connor play a couple of tunes, giving the professionals a chance to audition this unknown fiddler. When asked what he wanted to play, O'Connor responded with "Tom & Jerry," a particularly challenging fiddle tune. Randy says, "Charlie kinda cut his eyes up and looked at me as if to say, *either he's an idiot or he knows how to play a fiddle,* because 'Tom & Jerry,' that's not the tune you start out playing."

It was clear O'Connor knew how to play a fiddle. "He started off on the tune, and after the first chorus, Charlie was having a ball," Randy recalls. In fact, Collins was so impressed he told Randy to call Roy Acuff, a fan of good fiddle music, to come down and see the young fiddler. "So I called Roy," Randy says. "He was either in bed or getting ready to go to bed. He wanted to know who it was. I told him I didn't know; it was some young kid. But I told him he can handle a fiddle. When I said 'fiddle,' Roy said, 'Let me get dressed and I'll be down there in fifteen or twenty minutes.'" Randy also called Vassar Clements and Dr. Perry Harris, the coordinator of the Grand Masters Fiddlers Contest. Once Acuff arrived, he was so impressed with O'Connor that he brought the youngster onstage to play with him at the *Grand Ole Opry* the following Friday night. The next Monday, O'Connor found himself in a studio making his first recording and signing a recording contract. In O'Connor's own words: "Not bad for a first trip to Nashville!"

Early in his career, Charlie Daniels found a friend in Randy. The legendary fiddle player most famous for his hit "The Devil Went Down to Georgia" came to Nashville as a scruffy, relatively unknown musician. Randy implies Daniels could have easily been mistaken for a panhandler, saying, "We were always getting people coming in the store, looking for a handout or something. You know, you had panhandlers coming in all the time." Charlie Daniels first entered the Picking Parlor before he was widely recognized. Randy admits Daniels "would have been scary-looking to some people. . . . Charlie was a big boy, with long hair, a full beard, and he was dressed in buckskin." According to Randy, Daniels was in search of a new set of guitar strings. He told Randy he had just moved to town and was preparing for his first paying job—a session with the Earl Scruggs Revue. As the proverbial starving musician, he could not even afford a new set of strings for the session. Daniels promised to come back to the store and pay Randy after the gig if Randy would just loan him a set of strings. "Well, you know, we probably heard that story on average of three or four times a week," Randy claims. "Some people you helped out, and some people you didn't. It's just one of those things. There was something about Charlie. I said, 'Well, you know a set of strings ain't that much and to help the guy out maybe, and if it don't, well, ain't nothing much lost.'" Randy also knew Earl Scruggs and his sons Gary and Randy, who also played in the Revue. He knew they were discerning about who recorded with them. So Randy gave Daniels the strings.

Three or four weeks later, Daniels showed up again and repaid Randy for the set of guitar strings. "Hell, I'd probably given away a hundred sets of guitar strings to different people," Randy says. "But he was the only one who ever came back and paid me for them, like he said he would. After that, we became good friends."

Sometimes the Picking Parlor's impact was indirect, but meaningful nonetheless. The late Danny Gatton is remembered as a legendary electric guitar player. Yet he recalled feeling giddy during a pivotal encounter with one of his own heroes, Chet Atkins, at the Picking Parlor. Gatton appeared on an episode of the television show *Nashville Connection* and shared the experience with host Benny Dean, recalling:

> We'd have these jam sessions down there [at the Picking Parlor], Buddy Emmons would be there, and Buddy Spicher would play fiddle—just all kinds of people came in there. Chet came in there one night. Somebody told me he was there. I really didn't see him or know where he was, but I really got nervous; I got real scared. [Gatton describes how he was developing his own musical tone at the time.] Nothing really tricky, but just enough alteration in the sound that Chet was interested in what this was. So he came down to see it. That was a real thrill to get to meet him. (Danny Gatton interview n.d.)

The intermingling of musicians from all points on the ability spectrum made encounters such as Gatton's with Chet Atkins common.

For Mike Compton, the current torchbearer of Monroe-style mandolin playing, the Picking Parlor was "an oasis." Having just moved to Nashville from rural Mississippi, Compton found Nashville's size intimidating at first. But, he says, "Randy's place felt like home." Just like home, the Picking Parlor had its authority figure. Compton remembers that Randy was a "really imposing character. . . . He sort of looked like a 'Fonzie' kind of guy, with the way he wore his hair and his pointed sideburns." Yet there was something endearing about the imposing proprietor. "I felt at home around Randy," Compton says.

John McEuen's career arc was undoubtedly shaped by the Picking Parlor, even though he admits, "If I added it up, I probably didn't spend more than twenty hours there. But they were very important hours." As a kid in Southern California, McEuen spent time in McCabe's music store in Los Angeles, a shop that was to L.A. what the Picking Parlor was to Nashville. Describing his reaction to the Picking Parlor, McEuen says, "When I walked in there, I was at home." He adds, "People were sitting around playing, and it was a wide range of people. These were people that were coming to shop for instruments, or just coming in off the street, curious, or coming to get something fixed." The unusual combination of activities taking place within the confines of the Picking Parlor made sense to McEuen. "Randy was a guy that made banjo necks, and his name was Wood! What better thing? Even the word 'Randy' kinda fit—'Randy' meaning kind of like hard to figure out and goes his own direction and goes against the tide and does unexpected things. It was an unexpected thing for a guy with a music store to start having performers play there."

Today McEuen expresses deep gratitude for the opportunity to connect with Charlie Collins at the Picking Parlor. "He was a real guy. By 'real guy,' I mean that I'm an emulator. I came from Orange County, California. I was learning off rooms of records. I wasn't living the log cabin world. I was wanting to be there." Collins *had* been there. "I learned a lot of fiddle tunes from him. He knew them on the guitar. . . . He was very cordial, very nice. He provided a very good lesson on how to be, whether you're on stage or not," McEuen says.

To emphasize the importance of Collins's friendship, McEuen recalls a particular evening at the *Grand Ole Opry* when the Nitty Gritty Dirt Band was on the bill. Collins was a member of the house band at the *Opry*, and after the Dirt Band set, McEuen says, "Collins came up to me and said,

'Hey, John, do you want to bring that five-string out and back me up with a fiddle player and we can play for the square dancers?'" Given the success of the Dirt Band's *Circle* album at the time, it might have seemed beneath McEuen to play backup to a square dance. But McEuen claims, "*That* was one of the highest nights of my life at the *Opry*, because I *was* in 1948, playing the five-string banjo all below the fifth fret, backing up a fiddle player." McEuen acknowledges that the impactful friendship with Charlie Collins "developed because of Randy Wood and his cordiality of inviting people into his store to sit around and pick."

For the amateur, it was thrilling to be in the Picking Parlor, interacting with the professionals as though they were peers. Ed Foote remembers going there one day with the intention of selling a model 60D Dobro. When he got there, he saw a rare Martin O-18K Hawaiian-style guitar for sale on the showroom wall.

"Randy, how about I swap my Dobro for that?" Foote asked.

"Well, I don't know. There's a fair amount of Dobros around, but not many like this 18K," Randy said, reluctant to part with the guitar.

Foote persisted.

"OK, how about I put my Dobro on the wall right next to it with the same price? If somebody takes my Dobro, then I'll just take my Hawaiian home."

Randy agreed to the plan. "The very next day," Foote claims, "Hank Williams Jr. walks in, looking for a Dobro for his pedal steel player going out on tour. He took my Dobro, and Randy called me and said, 'Ed, come on down and get that Martin. I sold your Dobro.'" Foote was overjoyed to nab the instrument he coveted. The lore of the occasion was undoubtedly amplified by Williams's involvement in the deal. Referring to the Hawaiian guitar, Foote says, "I still have it. It's going to be a lifetime instrument."

Even Foote credits Randy with launching his career with a single sentence, uttered in Randy's slow Georgia drawl. After completing his training at the prestigious North Bennet Street Institute in Boston, Foote moved to Nashville to practice his trade as a piano tuner. He was hanging out in the Picking Parlor one afternoon when he happened to meet Harold Bradley, the Music Row studio cofounder. At the urging of a friend who was also present, Foote handed Bradley a calling card. "I was shy. I had never been in business before," Foote remembers. "I handed him my card, and Harold looked at it, and Harold looked at Randy and said, 'Randy, do you know anything about him?'" Randy replied, "I think he's a pretty good piano tuner." That's all it took.

The next day, Bradley was at a recording session when he encountered a problem with the studio piano. Unable to reach his usual piano tuner, he reached in his pocket for Foote's card and called him. It was a small break, but it was all Foote needed. "I hadn't just learned from the guy down the street," Foote says of his classical training. "My tuning was capable of going on any stage on the planet. These musicians had never heard a piano tuned that well. . . . The next day, a musician who had been at that session was in another studio and said, 'That piano doesn't really sound all that good.' I got a call. Just on the strength of Randy's word, all of a sudden, for the next eighteen years, I was the top-dollar tuner in this town."

"I did not realize how far Randy's influence extended," admits Foote. "For me, him telling Harold Bradley, 'I think he's a pretty good piano tuner' started my career in this town. I've thought later—that's credibility. Bradley was going strictly on faith. Since Randy said it was okay, this giant in the music industry took it on faith and said okay."

The Apprentices

The careers most heavily shaped by Randy Wood were those of his apprentices. Of course, Randy would have just called them his employees, but these young aspiring luthiers saw much more in the job than simply a source of income. It was good they did; apprenticeship was a meager source. "Complete poverty," as one former apprentice describes it, "but a fabulous job." Another, Chris Camp, described his reverence for landing a job working under Randy: "It was a magic time, and Randy was heading up the hippest spot in town."

Randy learned under the tutelage of Tut Taylor, and he has since made a point of not only delegating some of his workload to his employees but also imparting some of the knowledge he has acquired along the way. Because it is so hard to impress Randy, his apprentices hurled themselves into their work to earn his respect. A few words of praise from Randy Wood made up for a lot of scrawny paychecks.

Chris Camp was a fixture among the apprentices. Originally from New York, Camp had already taken an interest in building guitars when he took a vacation road trip to Nashville and found his way into the Picking Parlor. He was entranced by Randy and the whole scene. "I showed him my Polaroid pictures of a banjo neck I had just made and my first guitar that I had made without any guidelines or help," Camp recalls. He was eager to show Randy that he had some basic lutherie skills. He even mustered the courage to say he would like to work in Randy's shop. "You know how Randy is," Camp says about Randy's response. "He said, 'Well, I'll keep that in mind.' Then I was walking away like, *I think he hates me.*" Camp remembers leaving the Picking Parlor with three thoughts: "I'd love to go back there. Randy is pretty scary. And everybody can play really good!"

Camp returned to New York and tried to make a living as a musician, but he could not stop thinking about "this magic place where all of this stuff was happening" in Nashville. A couple of months later, he received a call from Coley Coleman, one of Randy's apprentices, who told Camp that Randy had a job opening and wondered if Camp would be interested in it. Of course, Camp jumped at the chance.

"Would I get to work in the shop?" Camp asked.

"Don't get ahead of yourself," Coleman replied. "What Randy has in mind is that you could be the shop punching bag . . . the low man on the totem pole. Fifty bucks a week, and whatever work you can find. As soon as you can find some repair work, you can start getting some money from repairs."

With that offer, the twenty-four-year-old Camp packed up his robin's-egg-blue VW squareback and drove seventeen hours from New York to Nashville.

"I started my job there with him," Camp says, "and there's really no job description. There are no guidelines. You're just there." What does a new, eager employee do in the absence of a clear job description? He looks for an opportunity. "Of course," Camp explains, "I immediately looked around and thought, *This place is a mess. This place looks like a bomb went off.*" He continues, "The first month I was there, I made the mistake of cleaning. I cleaned the tool room from top to bottom. I organized the lumber; I swept the floor. Immediately afterward, it looked like a bomb went off again."

In time, Camp earned his own bench where he repaired and built instruments. The path to that point was educational and humbling. "One of Randy's teaching methods," Camp explains, "was that he didn't really give you instructions and say, 'Here's how you do this.' He let you learn by trial and error. But he'd almost send you down the wrong path to see if you'd notice." Camp was a mere nine years younger than Randy, but "at that point in my life," he says, "Randy looked like he was a lot older than me. He looked like a four-star general, and I was a buck private." Camp remembers a common exchange he and Randy would have: "Randy would come over to me . . . lumbering over, and I'm like the little mouse in the cartoon, the bookkeeper, cowering."

"I don't know how you can get anything done," Randy would say.

"Randy, what are you talking about?"

"You're too busy putting everything away, and now I can't find anything."

Camp now acknowledges, "Randy knew where everything was that wasn't put away."

Randy gave Camp more than just a job. "Randy gave me the opportunity to be in the fabric of Nashville before it shifted gears," he says. He remembers that musicians from all over the country would come to Nashville, and one of their first priorities would be to find Randy. Camp recalls seeing a teenager bound into the shop and start chatting with Randy. "Randy comes over to me later, and he says, 'Come on over here. I want you to meet somebody.' He introduces me to this young guy. He says, 'This kid's gonna be a big star. He's a great musician, talented mandolin player.'" The young musician was Ricky Skaggs. "That kind of thing just kept happening. Every week, someone amazing came in looking for Randy." Chris Camp eventually left his apprenticeship at the Old Time Picking Parlor to launch his own career as a luthier in Southern California.

According to Randy, his "most famous apprentice" was Danny Ferrington, "a little ol' short guy with more energy than anybody needs," Randy claims. Anyone who knows Ferrington can attest to his enthusiastic joie de vivre and his rapid-fire cadence when talking. Ferrington may have been raised in a small town in Louisiana, but he had big-city ambitions. Randy helped him bring them to fruition. Ferrington learned woodworking skills from his father, who owned a cabinet shop. Ferrington also visited the woodshop of a man in Monroe named Doc Savage. Savage happened to be a friend of Randy's. "Doc would buy guitar bodies that had a little bit of damage, and he'd get tops and necks, and stick them on and put his name on them," explains Ferrington. "So he always stopped in Nashville and went by the Picking Parlor." Ferrington was in Savage's shop one day when Randy called and told Savage he was looking for some more help at the Picking Parlor. Savage told Randy about Ferrington, and Randy invited Danny to Nashville to interview for the position. Ferrington made the trip up to Nashville—his first—and met Randy to discuss the specifics of the job. He recalls that the pay would be two dollars an hour. "I went back home to Louisiana thinking about it," Ferrington remembers. "I didn't want to leave home . . . but Nashville was an appealing thing to me. There were musicians. I liked playing music; I didn't want to make a career playing music, necessarily, but I liked being around it." After giving the job offer some thought, he realized, "I don't have any life experiences. . . . I'm twenty-three years old, still living at home." To a young, untraveled Louisianan, Randy's offer was like an "apple dangled in front of your face," Ferrington says. "It was an opportunity, and I didn't have to figure out a way to make that opportunity happen. It was just there. So I moved up there in July 1975." It was tough for him to leave home, though. "I cried all the way."

As soon as Ferrington arrived in Nashville, he knew he had made the right decision. "When I actually got up there, I felt as if I had gone to bluegrass heaven" (Schell 1992). He was surrounded by musicians that, until his move, he had only read about. Ferrington, a natural extrovert, also made close friendships soon after arriving. "I got into a whole family role with them up there," he says. And of course, he honed his lutherie skills under the Randy Wood teaching method. "Randy would let me do things because he didn't want to do them. It was less of Randy training me; more of just doing the kind of job he wasn't interested in doing." But this was hardly distasteful to the wide-eyed Nashville newcomer. "It was great because it gave me a chance to learn and work on more famous guitars than I would have normally gotten to on my own, because they were funneled through Randy." Ferrington reserves high praise for the impact Randy had on his eventual career as a luthier. "I learned almost everything I know from him. . . . Randy was a man of few words, but he had a kind of magical touch when it came to wood, and he was generous with his knowledge." Ferrington remembers fondly a typical evening at the Picking Parlor: "Randy would go up in the shop and just let them play music downstairs, and Irene would run the club. He would just come upstairs and work by himself in the shop. I'd go up there and hang out with Randy. It was a really nice time. The light was good. You could hear the music downstairs. It was terrific."

It was not always peaceful upstairs, though. Randy was a skilled rifle builder as well as a luthier, and Ferrington recalls, "Randy and [apprentice] Jim Johnson would sight their rifles in next door while we were working." The process of sighting involved aiming the rifle at a target and actually shooting at the target to determine any alignment error and correct it appropriately. The upper floor of the Picking Parlor was divided into two spaces in the early years; the workshop occupied one space, and the other was left vacant. A sliding metal door separated the two. At one end of the vacant space, Randy kept a tree stump that became his target. "[He] and Jim would make these Tennessee long rifles, you know, flint lock . . . beautiful," Ferrington recalls. "He and Jim would go next door and sight 'em *in the building*! So if you had opened the door and stuck your head in there, you'd have gotten a bullet in your head! That was the kinda crazy shit they would do. They just thought that was completely normal—shooting a gun in the building." When questioned about this, Randy admits, "There were a few times we touched a few rounds off in the building. . . . You probably couldn't hardly hear it outside. That was pretty much a warehouse district. The neighbor on one side was a moving company, and they used that building just to store goods. The other building was a gay nightclub, so there was nobody there during the day."

Whereas Randy criticized Chris Camp for spending too much time cleaning up, he tried to persuade Danny to slow down. "He was a real good repairman and a pretty good builder," Randy says in his characteristically muted way. "He tried to be too fast. He built a guitar for Paul Craft one time—built it in like three days. And he started to string it up, and it just exploded, because the glue wasn't dry." Ferrington actually agrees with Randy's opinion of his own working style. "Randy's critique of me always was that I'd be good if I just slowed down. . . . He was completely right, but what am I going to do? You are who you are." That did not stop Ferrington from appreciating Randy's technique. He admired his "economy of motion" and says that he and his fellow apprentices "were frustrated to be able to do in a day what he could do in just a couple of moves."

Randy has a history of being drawn to people quite different from himself. His friendship with George Gruhn is one case in point. Danny Ferrington, with his energy, excitability, and extroversion, is another. Yet the two enjoyed each other's company. "Danny was the kind of people that everybody liked," Randy says. Ferrington reciprocates the sentiment. "It's a funny thing. I've sort of gravitated to guys like Randy, who were opposite from my personality. I like big, quiet teddy bears. I know who they are. They don't scare me. Some people were kind of intimidated by Randy; they couldn't figure him out. I know those kind of guys instantly. I don't know why that was built into me, but I've always had huge friends. Big lugs and quiet kind of guys like that. I love 'em. And they love me. Me and Randy got along instantly. We never had a thing where *oh, I grew to understand Randy.* I knew Randy the minute I met him."

Danny Ferrington had a weakness for celebrities of film and song alike. Randy remembers that "Danny was a huge *Star Wars* fan. He saw *Star Wars* when he was working for me, and I couldn't get no work out of him for like two days, he was so blown away. When it came to town, I mean, he was the first guy in line to see that." Later Ferrington fell completely under the spell of one of music's biggest celebrities of that era, Linda Ronstadt. "Danny was in love with Linda Ronstadt," Randy recalls. "He just was crazy about Linda. I've never seen anybody so crazy." Fortunately for Ferrington, he had a job that brought him close to celebrities. He actually found an opportunity to meet Ronstadt one evening when she was at a music club several blocks away from the Picking Parlor. "When he heard she was over there," Randy remembers, "he ran because that was faster than driving." Ferrington was awestruck. After her performance, he invited her to come back to the Picking Parlor. But after running back to share the news that she would be arriving, he found Randy at the end of a work day, tired and ready to go home. "We were getting ready to close up, and everybody was already gone, and we were getting ready to lock the door," Randy says.

"You can't close up now!" Ferrington exclaimed.

"We're already closed up. Why can't we close?"

"Well, Linda Ronstadt's gonna get on stage and sing for us!"

"Well, not tonight she ain't."

Randy says, "Danny was plum beside himself because we wouldn't open back up."

After working at the Picking Parlor for several years, it was clear Danny wanted a faster pace of life than he could find working under Randy. Ferrington concluded that Nashville was too small for him. He needed peers and customers who were not so traditional. "The bluegrassers are not going to buy a guitar from me," he admits about his guitar designs. He experimented with nontraditional shapes and sizes for his guitars. Few of them resembled the Martin dreadnaughts so cherished by die-hard bluegrass fans. But while he was working for Randy, he hustled, actively developing his own following. "I was getting on an airplane and flying to England," Danny says of his efforts to market himself. "Randy wouldn't drive up to Music Row. I was going to concerts with Journey and Eagles, standing around being humiliated to go backstage and show these guys stuff. I was getting orders Randy was never going to get.... I went to England twice. I was taking guitars with me. I'd take slides, and I had a little slide viewer. I flew on the Concorde back from England, because I had sold two guitars to Justin Hayward of Moody Blues, and Eric Clapton ordered two. So I had sold four guitars, and I was sittin' rich." It is easy to assume Randy would have harbored some resentment in the midst of Ferrington's self-promotional activity, but remarkably he did not. "He was always completely supportive."

Ferrington eventually moved to Los Angeles and became a West Coast ambassador for bluegrass music. He set up shop in a garret he rented above an automotive paint store. When the store was closed, he slipped in and out of his shop by shimmying up and down a rope dangling down the side of the building and crawling through an open window. He later moved his shop to a more conventional ground floor garage in Santa Monica. The shop hosted a wide array of Hollywood luminaries he has befriended. He invited them over to visit and simply soak in the sights and smells of a woodshop. He also infused his visitors with folk and bluegrass music from records that filled shelf after shelf around the walls of his work space. Movie producer Ethan Coen was a repeat visitor. "We come here to the shop, and we pick," Ferrington boasts in his shop. "We are good pals." In fact, the Coen brothers commissioned Ferrington to build the instruments that appeared in the movie *The Ladykillers*. During one visit to the shop, Danny explains that Coen told him, "We're doing a movie with old bluegrassy, rootsy kind of music, and country kind of music—stuff that you like. You'll have to play me some stuff." Danny eagerly pulled down vinyl records from his massive collection on the shelves lining his shop walls. "I went through Ralph Stanley, Bill Monroe-y kind of stuff," Ferrington explains. He continued through the catalogs of bluegrass luminaries he had met in Nashville, such as Vassar Clements and Norman Blake. That movie with bluegrassy, rootsy music became *O Brother, Where Art Thou?*, a film that catapulted bluegrass into the consciousness of a new generation of fans.

Randy on the Big and Small Screen

Back in Nashville in the 1970s, Randy Wood did not long for Hollywood fame. But he and the Old Time Picking Parlor became such Nashville fixtures that both the man and the venue were featured on television and film when directors needed to emphasize the Music City as a setting in their plotlines.

On October 1, 1972, *The Nashville Coyote* premiered on television as part of the *Wonderful World of Disney* series, a testimony to the country's fascination with Nashville at that time. The hourlong show follows the ramblings of a western coyote named Chico, who hops into an open railroad box car to nap, only to wake up and find his box car now sitting in a rail yard near Nashville. Chico's plight is intertwined with the story of a down-and-out songwriter named Johnny Martin, played by Walter

Forbes. Martin is seeking stardom by pitching his songs to Music Row record companies, but he keeps striking out. After a series of rejections, he wanders into a park and sees a group of pickers playing and singing under the shade of a large tree. The group, called the Nashville Losers Club, is fronted by Randy Wood, playing guitar and singing, "You Can't Go in the Red Playing Bluegrass."

The Nashville Losers Club consisted of Randy, Vassar Clements on fiddle, Tom McKinney on banjo, Norman Blake on mandolin, and Tut Taylor on Dobro. It was an impressive lineup of bluegrass talent. In fact, it was such a skilled group of professionals that even the show's producer hardly believed they could record their scene in one take. "We went in the studio and recorded the thing," Randy says, referring to the music track that was dubbed over the video, "then a couple weeks later we went out to location to shoot it. . . . They had set aside six hours to do this thing—just one damn song! And we said, 'Hell, it ain't gonna take longer than ten minutes!'" Serious session musicians in Nashville earn their living by getting it right in one take, but this young producer was skeptical. With cameras rolling, Randy and the other musicians pantomimed their song, playing their instruments and singing to the previously recorded track. When the song concluded, Randy thought they were done. They were surprised when the producer told them he needed a few more takes because, as Randy recalls hearing the producer say, "Nobody can do that on one take." Apparently this group could. "We wound up doing it four different times, and he still used the first take. All day, he's shaking his head because he's used to Hollywood actors, and they can't get nothing right on the first time around."

In the show, Johnny Martin, seeing the high level of musicianship that only constitutes "loser" status in Nashville, tosses his precious original songs in a trash can and drives back home out West. Chico the coyote fares no better in Nashville. He finds himself in an open field during a fox hunt and is pursued by a pack of barking hounds. As he is fleeing, Chico sees Martin and leaps in the car to go back home, too.

In the movie, the narrator claims the losers "couldn't get an audience among the local music moguls, but the girlfriends and wives could always be counted on." Among the wives who could be counted on sat Irene Wood, wearing a long-sleeved white sweater, flashing a big smile, with her hands around her knees and her blonde hair up in vintage 1970s style. Her role in the cast turned out to be more demanding than she originally realized, as Randy explains. "They had a little audience sitting out on the grass, and this was August or September, you know, a nice time. Well, long about first of December, they discovered that there wasn't something right about the scene, so we had to go back and do it. There was about two inches of snow on the ground." Most of the on-screen audience had worn clothes appropriate for early fall during the first round of filming, and they had to put those same clothes back on to reshoot the scene. The weather had turned much colder, though. "So here we are out there—fortunately I had worn a sweater, so I wasn't in too bad a shape. But Tut and them liked to froze their ass off. And Irene . . . she liked to died. . . . It was cold as hell out there that day."

Movie audiences were treated to a glimpse of life in the Picking Parlor on the big screen when Robert Altman's film *Nashville* hit theaters in 1975. The film covers five days of life in Nashville, as experienced by an eclectic array of twenty-four characters, from country music stars to housewives, and businessmen to gypsies. With frequent scene-hopping among the interwoven storylines of the characters, *Nashville* is at once a comedy, a political satire, a drama, and a musical with more than an hour of cumulative performance footage. The film boasts an impressive cast including Ned Beatty, Lily Tomlin, Jeff Goldblum, and Elliott Gould. The film received wide praise by critics. It was nominated for five Academy Awards, including Best Picture. Altman chose iconic locations in Nashville for settings in the movie, and one of those locations was the Picking Parlor.

In one segment, two scenes from Nashville nightlife are juxtaposed. One setting is a dark, half-empty bar, and the other is the Picking Parlor, bursting with patrons enjoying the bluegrass sounds of the house band, the Misty Mountain Boys. The atmosphere in the Picking Parlor is lively. Listeners crowd around the gingham-tablecloth-topped tables, and an overflow crowd lines the walls. The joy in the scene is short-lived, though. A bar fight begins over a racial slur and spills out onto the dark sidewalk, concluding the brief scene.

Sharp-eyed viewers can spot Irene Wood, with her bright blonde hair, behind the bar as the camera pans the room. Randy was present in some scenes while shooting took place, but ultimately he did not make the final cut. "What little bit I did wound up on the cutting room floor," he says with a laugh.

Randy had little patience for the hoopla surrounding film production. As he had learned during the filming of *The Nashville Coyote*, only a fraction of footage actually makes it into the final version. The Picking Parlor scene in *Nashville* lasts less than five minutes, but Randy recalls, "They kept the Picking Parlor tied up for three days and then there was a fourth day that we couldn't do anything because they had damn cables and shit running out the doors because they were filming right out in front of the Picking Parlor for an afternoon and into the evening.... They must have had ten to twelve eighteen-wheelers just for production." Randy was dumbfounded by the scale of the production. However, Altman probably did not consider it excessive. Randy remembers, "When they cut the damn thing, Robert told everybody, 'That's it. I've cut everything out of it I can possibly cut out of it and still tell the story. That's it.' Well, when they put it all together, it was still like four and a half hours long, so they wound up cutting some more off it." The film still clocks in at a lengthy two hours and thirty-eight minutes.

While Randy may trivialize his participation in the movie, the Picking Parlor's presence in *Nashville* continues to be a feather in his cap. Altman's decision to include the Picking Parlor in his film validates the favored-venue status that Randy's place enjoyed in its heyday.

After getting a taste of television and film with *Nashville Coyote* and *Nashville*, Randy was happy to settle back into his niche in the music business. "Those were the only two I had any direct thing with," he says, referring to the movies. "I basically said, 'If that's what movie-making is about, they can have it.'"

Instruments

The craft of woodworking was always the foundation of the business at the Old Time Picking Parlor. While patrons sought musical inspiration, Randy inspired many with his intuitive sense of craftsmanship. Ed Foote, one of Randy's disciples, claims, "What a lot of people don't fully appreciate about Randy is how good he is with his hands. It's not just musical instruments. I've seen him make a box for a pistol, and by the end of the week, he had this box with hand-carved feet on it, all meshed together. It was just absolutely perfect." Foote earned the privilege of dabbling in the workshop alongside the apprentices and saw the depth of Randy's skill. "He watched me clamp a piece of wood up, taking a file trying to true the joint up," Foote recalls. "He said, 'Un-uh, don't do that. Hold it in your hand, so you can make the wood fit to that file. If you clamp it up, you're going to put a bevel on it.' Feel the material—that was his whole thing. And that's what he does." Foote confesses, "I don't know enough about guitar construction to know if his instruments were good or not, but I know the craftsmanship that went into them was just staggering."

Randy's reputation afforded him opportunities to work on unique instruments. One was a small guitar belonging to Andrew Jackson's estate at the seventh U.S. president's Tennessee plantation, the Hermitage. "It was Rachel Jackson's guitar. It needed some work. It had some cracks on it, and stuff needed tightening up just to preserve it, so they asked me to do that," Randy says, as if the job were just one more task in his daily queue. He is equally unemotional when he explains that he inlaid a small rectangle of mother-of-pearl engraved with the letters C-A-S-H to cover a hole in the top of the D-45 belonging to Johnny Cash. J. T. Gray remembers that Randy inlaid a design on a guitar for Emmylou Harris. She "still plays a J-200 that Randy inlaid a red rose on it for her," he says. Unfortunately, Randy rarely documented these projects that would have such visibility later. "Like a lot of stuff that I did, I didn't think about taking pictures of nothin'. I was too busy tryin' to make a living," Randy declares.

That humility endeared him to many of Nashville's greats. When the father of bluegrass music, Bill Monroe, needed to tend to his mandolin, he turned to Randy Wood for care. It is not an exaggeration to claim that no other instrument has impacted an entire genre the way Bill Monroe's mandolin did for bluegrass music. That sound, heard on rural stages and broadcast across the night sky on the waves of WSM, launched bluegrass, and "Randy's the only guy who Monroe would let work on his instrument," according to John Hedgecoth.

Monroe's main mandolin was a 1923 Gibson F-5 he reportedly found in a barber shop in Miami, Florida, in 1946. Initially, Monroe sent the instrument back to Gibson when it needed repair. "The story I got from him," Randy says of Monroe, "was that right after he got it, the frets were worn out on it, and it needed new frets. He sent it back to Gibson because nobody was doing fret repair work. Instead of putting new frets on it, they just yanked the old board off there and put a new fingerboard on it.... So he had it in his mind that you couldn't replace the frets; you had to replace the fingerboard." With Monroe's tireless playing schedule and his aggressive playing style, he quickly wore down new frets. "Monroe had a grip like a mule in his left hand," Randy says. "He could, just by sheer force, get a note out of it, even though the frets were gone." Monroe again sent the mandolin to Gibson for fret repair. "That was the primary reason Monroe had sent that mandolin back to Gibson back when they messed it up," Randy says of the worn frets. The "mess-up" would become part of Bill Monroe lore. When Gibson received Monroe's mandolin, the company decided that such a highly visible product of theirs needed refurbishment. The repair shop applied a new finish to the well-worn mandolin. "Well, as we all know, that was the wrong thing to do," Randy says. Monroe resented Gibson for destroying the original finish of his mandolin. He was so upset that he carved the "Gibson" out of the "The Gibson" nameplate on the headstock with his pocket knife, leaving only the "The" remaining. It became a defining feature of his storied mandolin.

After that episode with Gibson, Monroe turned to Randy exclusively for care of his mandolin. When the frets became worn, Monroe again assumed he needed a full fretboard replacement. Randy tried to explain that the fingerboard could be planed and salvaged, and only the frets needed replacing. "No, he didn't want it refretted. He wanted a new fret board, because that was the only way you could fix it—he had that in his mind. So, being Monroe, you did what Monroe wanted done." Randy duly complied. Not long after, Monroe's frets needed another replacement. "So he brought it in, and I told him again, I said, 'We don't need to replace this board. I can take those frets out, clean the board up, put new frets in, and you'll never know the difference.'" Monroe agreed to give it a try.

"He still didn't quite believe me, but he was willing to try it." It was that repair that gave birth to an apocryphal tale that has followed Randy ever since. "There's a story that goes around, and it has some validity, that he told me to take it home and sleep with it," Randy jokes. The truth is not far from that.

When Monroe brought the mandolin to Randy, he asked, "You're gonna be the one working on it, right?"

"Yes, sir. I'll take good care of it."

"Just to be sure, why don't you take it home with you every evening?"

According to Randy's memory of the exchange, "That was pretty much all he said, but the story got out that he told me to take it home and put it under my bed every night. Of course, I didn't take it home. It was safer there at the shop than it was at my house, especially driving back and to." Randy refretted the mandolin, and since "the pearl nut was just worn down to nothing," he also replaced the nut. Monroe played it for about a week before bringing it back to Randy, complaining that the instrument did not feel right. "He wanted to know what all I had done, so I told him. He said, 'Put my old nut back on it.' So I built it up, I had to shim it. I put it on there, and he was happy with it."

As impressionable as Monroe's F-5 was to budding mandolinists, Tony Rice's 1935 Martin D-28 has had a similar effect on a generation of flatpick guitar players. A devoted student of the Byrds' guitarist Clarence White, Rice had an opportunity to buy White's dreadnaught after White was struck by a car and killed. But before Rice played the guitar on stage, he had to make one stop first. "When I got it . . . it was a wreck. The first thing I had done was to take it to Randy Wood," Rice recounted in an interview with *Flatpicking Guitar Magazine* (Kimsey 1998). In his biography, *Still Inside*, Rice says, "Two weeks after I got it back to Lexington, I drove it down to Randy Wood. Randy re-set the neck and planed the fingerboard, re-fretted it, re-bound it, put a new bridge on it, and did a bunch of stuff to get it to where it would look and play good" (Stafford and Wright 2010). From the musician's perspective, he got what he wanted: his guitar in good playing order. Randy remembers sweating out the "bunch of stuff" he had to squeeze into this last-minute repair job. "When Tony got that guitar, he was still playing with the Bluegrass Alliance," Randy recalls. "He popped up at the Picking Parlor at, like, nine-thirty one morning. He was just so excited, he couldn't hardly talk." Rice was in love with the instrument, but it needed plenty of work. "It needed a neck set, it needed a new fingerboard, a new bridge, and maybe there was a brace or two loose in it, I don't recall, but I know it was all major work."

Randy said to Rice, "I'd love to do it . . . but we're looking at a couple of weeks' worth of work here."

"I gotta play this thing tonight," Rice replied.

"Man, there ain't no way you can do that."

"Well, you've got to."

"I'll see what I can do."

The guitar was unique for its long fingerboard and lack of inlay dots. So stock repair items would not work for this job. "I had to start basically from scratch," Randy says. "I had to make a fingerboard from a blank, saw the frets. And I had to make a bridge, because those were wider spaced bridges, and you couldn't get that from Martin. But I reset the neck, made that fingerboard, put it on, and made a new bridge and put it on." Rice was in a hurry to get to his next gig, and he needed to leave Nashville that afternoon. Randy continues: "So we got all that glued up, and I had glued the bridge on, like, an hour earlier. I took the clamps off and put strings on it and got it set up to where I knew the action was going to be good, and I got the nut cut and everything. Then we took the strings loose and put the clamps back on the bridge, and he took the guitar that way and took it on up to Louisville or wherever it was. And it was like thirty minutes before time to go on, he took the clamps off of it, strung it up, and got it tuned up and all. He said everything held together." The guitar has been in Rice's arsenal for most of his pioneering recordings.

In its prime, the Old Time Picking Parlor was one of Nashville's most popular destinations for a fan of bluegrass and country music. And it achieved this with a notable lack of pretentiousness. Destitute pickers could walk in and jam with music legends, in a relaxed setting with folksy decor, complete with picnic tablecloths and a pot-bellied stove. The place achieved its magic because it avoided taking itself too seriously. "We were just trying to make a livin'," Randy says. "We weren't thinking about history" (T. Wood 2009). But Randy wanted the Picking Parlor to grow. The crowds showing up nightly for live music convinced him that he had limitless growth potential. However, his pursuit of that growth would prove that the template for the Picking Parlor's success was a fragile one.

PICKING PARLOR SUNSET

Nashville, from my point of view, has served its purpose.

RANDY WOOD

Nashville in the Late 70s

While Nashville benefited from the commercial success of country music, there were some growing pains along the way. Randy began to feel them in the mid- to late 1970s.

Most notable was the *Grand Ole Opry*'s move out of the Ryman Auditorium. While the Ryman was revered as the "Mother Church of Country Music," it was never known for its comforts. Audience members sat in hard pews with tight legroom, and its lack of air conditioning meant artists and audience members suffered in the sweltering heat Nashville experiences in the summer months. In 1974 the *Opry* moved to the Grand Ole Opry House, a modern, spacious auditorium east of downtown. Performers and patrons appreciated the space, seat padding, and air conditioning, but the new venue drew one of Nashville's main attractions away from downtown.

Country music's identity crisis issues were stoked when Olivia Newton-John won the CMA award for Female Vocalist of the Year. Many country purists considered her to be an unequivocal pop singer who was overstepping her bounds with her airplay on country radio. That the CMA, an association with the mission of preserving the identity of country music, would give a pop artist such a prestigious honor rankled many.

Those who felt betrayed by the direction of the music business in Nashville found some solace in the "Outlaw" movement that had begun with Willie Nelson and Waylon Jennings. As proof of the growing popular-ity of the movement, a 1976 RCA compilation album *Wanted: the Outlaws* that included songs by Nelson and Jennings sold over one million copies (Malone 2010, 404). The Outlaw movement conjured images of Western scenes more readily found in Texas than in the urban center of Nashville.

Bluegrass was also coming off the wave of popularity following the 1972 *Circle* album. Flatt and Scruggs had split in 1969, and enough time had passed that rising music fans in the late 1970s did not come of age with the same reverence for the band's importance. Younger audiences were finding a new form of music, southern rock, to maintain some sense of identity with southern heritage. Artists such as Graham Parsons, Charlie Daniels, ZZ Top, Lynard Skynard, and the Allman Brothers epitomized this emerging genre (Malone 2010, 388).

In the midst of these changes, Doug Green, writing his 1976 *Pickin' Magazine* article, saw some clouds on the horizon for the Picking Parlor. He describes the "rapidly declining nature of the lower Broadway area of Nashville in which [Randy] is located." While deteriorating surroundings may have concerned Randy, this phenomenon hardly seemed a threat to his existence in Nashville. Apparently Green underestimated the pres-sure mounting on Randy—pressure that originated not in the surround-ing neighborhood but within the walls of the Picking Parlor. Within two years, Randy would reach the breaking point, and his time in Nashville would be over.

The external pressures that Green observed were real enough. Green felt they were "perhaps Randy's only serious problem." He explained that "when the *Opry* was broadcast from the Ryman Auditorium, only three blocks away at Fifth and Broadway, the area consisted of cut-rate furniture stores, low-rent 'souvenir' stores, and a few nationally known landmarks like Tootsie's Orchid Lounge, Sho-Bud, Ernest Tubb's Records Shop, Linebaugh's Restaurant, and Roy Acuff's Museum." In other words, there were a few respectable neighbors, at least. But by 1976, "tacky [had] turned tawdry, with friendly neighborhood porno stores and massage parlors taking over where *Opry* tourist exploiters once ruled, and while the area is losing some of its old flavor, it is gaining a new, much gamier, one" (Green 1976).

Randy remained optimistic. As the prime promoter of the Picking Parlor, he had to be. "I don't think it will really deteriorate that much," he says regarding the neighborhood in the *Pickin'* article. He elaborates, predicting that "Nashville will someday wake up, and this will be a restored historic area, full of shops and offices in these old buildings." With his rosy forecast for his commercial neighborhood, he boldly declared to Green, "I've ruled out moving." He was even thinking about how he could position himself to thrive when Nashville would finally wake up and flock to lower Broadway. "I'm trying to figure out some way to redo this building that will be financially and structurally sound." He could not have imagined he was unwittingly figuring out his own demise in Nashville.

The Picking Parlor Renovation

Hindsight has given wisdom to many who followed the life of the Old Time Picking Parlor. Nearly everyone's analysis leads to the same conclusion: the Picking Parlor renovation signaled the beginning of the end of Randy's magic era in the Music City.

The renovation was an ambitious project. Randy knocked out the wall between the music store and club to create one large room occupying the entire ground floor. From the day it opened, the Picking Parlor had occupied two store fronts. The ground floor of one side consisted of the music store. Walls of instruments attracted the eye of visitors walking in the front door. The intimate jam sessions grabbed the ears of people still outside on the sidewalk. The other half of the ground floor was the music club. It was long and narrow, which made it a cozy listening room. After renovation, Randy moved the music store—and the main draw for jamming musicians—upstairs. He relocated the repair shop in the vacant space upstairs where he had formerly sighted his long rifles.

Danny Ferrington remembers, "Randy thought he would compete with the other big clubs and get bigger acts. Randy wanted to get a big room to compete with the Exit Inn," referring to another popular music club in Nashville. In retrospect, Ferrington observes, "He just overstepped his bounds. You have got to have such a turnover at a place like that. You've got to be selling lots of liquor. It's got to become a real hangout place. He never cemented it."

As always, money was tight, and Randy had to be resourceful to execute his planned expansion. As noted previously, he called on his friend Buck White to put dormant plumbing skills to work. Randy recalls, "When we got ready to do the remodeling on the Picking Parlor, one of the main things we had to do was put in some bathrooms, because we had one little ol' bathroom in there for the whole dang place. So rather than go out and hire a big plumbing company, I just hired Buck. I'm sure he gave me a good deal on it."

A 1976 article in the *Tennessean* heralds the "major physical renovation" at the Old Time Picking Parlor while simultaneously sending distress signals to longtime patrons. The article describes the new listening room that is "twice the space as before—seating capacity, 200. A wall, a set of stairs and the old bar have come down, exposing an old staircase on either side of a new stage and the original brick wall of the building." But the article also warns, "Old time Picking Parlor patrons won't recognize the surroundings." Even the menu changed, with the addition of "mixed drinks and wine . . . to the usual beer and pizza." The article summarizes the changes as "startling" (Harvey 1976). It was an ominous word choice.

Randy had a reasonable motivation for embarking on the project. "During the summer, especially, we were turning away more people than we were seating," he tells the *Tennessean*. He was confident the public's enthusiasm for the original business model meant there was demand for bigger performances at the Picking Parlor. He saw the potential for big-name talent, but he says, "We couldn't begin to afford that with the seating capacity we had before." The article concludes with a foreboding quote from Randy: "We'll make it one of these days, maybe."

Many of the Picking Parlor's biggest fans were indeed startled by the renovation project, just as the *Tennessean* had predicted. John Hedgecoth admonishes Randy for messing with the Picking Parlor's secret sauce, saying:

> You don't mess with something that's so good and so magic. It was working perfectly like it was. Randy closed the doors of the music club for like three or four months at least to renovate. All these people that were coming from out of town with their friends, telling their

friends, 'You won't believe this place, it's incredible,' they showed up and the doors are closed. So all of that crowd quit coming. Then when the place reopened, it was this huge cavernous music room. It was too big and too impersonal to fill up. The old club was real intimate and cheery, and everybody felt at home there. The new club was huge and dark. And the music store—the picking room that was downstairs and you could see from the street—that was gone. It kinda lost the magic somehow."

Looking back on that time, J. T. Gray agrees with Hedgecoth. Gray was there in the early days when the Picking Parlor steadily built a loyal crowd of bluegrass fans. "During that time that he was down and remodeling, we lost that crowd," Gray says. "It's hard to explain what happened, except that we just lost our regular crowd that was coming beforehand. And then, after the remodel, it made it a little bit more on the modern edge. He went to a full bar. Before, it was just draft beer and pizza . . . and everybody loved it." The Picking Parlor, in its original layout, sported a charm that Gray liked. "A lot of people were sad to see it change," he says, reflecting his own sentiments as much as others'. "But I guess at that time, Randy had a vision of things being better if he remodeled, and a few more people would come in." Hedgecoth and Gray may have accurately reflected the mood of the patrons, but Randy saw an opportunity for greater prosperity.

Apprentice Chris Camp appreciates the pull that Randy felt. "There's this terrible motivation that you gotta expand and you gotta grow. It looks like a good idea, and you go for it. But you just double your square footage, and everything grows exponentially," he says recognizing the challenges associated with business growth. Echoing the thoughts of others, Camp says, "When the club got big, the nightly bluegrass vibe evaporated. It went over to the Station Inn and a couple of other clubs that were really for the bluegrassers."

The loss of the original vibe forced Randy to take actions that now appear to have exacerbated the problem. With a larger venue, Randy reached out for acts that might appeal to a broader audience. Of course, those big acts were expensive, and Randy had to fill more seats to cover the cost. "It became unmanageable as soon as it got that big," Camp says. "Too much square footage, too many considerations, too much overhead, not enough of the right people."

After the renovation, the *Tennessean* published another article in May 1977 indicating the Picking Parlor was flagging, grasping at straws to return to its glory days. In "Parlor: Back to Bluegrass," it is clear Randy is losing steam. Reporter Laura Eipper finds Randy in the sad position of admitting the new format is not working. His last option was to attempt a return to bluegrass. "It's been a hard decision to make, but I think it's the only thing I can do. The Picking Parlor is something Nashville needs, but I can't afford to give it to people all by myself." Eipper describes how attempts to draw crowds by booking big-name country acts often yielded "a disappointingly half-filled room." Randy is quoted grumbling, "In other markets like New York or Los Angeles, labels heavily support listening rooms, but here they don't and you have the additional problem of a smaller population. . . . Maybe it's the case of the cobbler's children having no shoes—people who are around music all day just don't want to be bothered with it after work" (Eipper, 1977).

Failed Franchise Attempt

Doug Green picked up on another dream of Randy's: franchising the Picking Parlor. Franchising was another dream that, like the renovation, teased Randy with visions of riches. "I would like to open Old Time Pickin' Parlors in other towns—the club part, that is. I couldn't keep up with the repair and custom work!" he tells Green in *Pickin'*. Randy had an optimistic assessment of the demand for bluegrass across the country. He tells Green: "Nashville, of course, has about four places that support it, and Louisville has always been a good Bluegrass town, with at least a couple places that book it pretty steadily. Atlanta has had some success, and I think even Birmingham has or has had a Bluegrass club. Knoxville, Cincinnati . . . there are a lot of possibilities. I don't think it's something you can get rich at, but it would be a real good thing for me and for Bluegrass music" (Green 1976). Like the renovation, the franchise pursuit would deal an already weary Randy another discouraging blow.

The apprentices noticed Randy's gaze had turned toward the nightclub side of the business and away from woodworking—the craft that had been the foundation of Randy's reputation. Chris Camp says, "Randy was transitioning into really wanting to promote the nightclub and making his tripod concept work with the nightclub, the music store, and the instrument shop." Danny Ferrington noticed Randy "always had this dream of being a rich club owner." But a large, successful club needs promotion, and Randy has always found more fulfillment as a craftsman than as a promoter.

As with Randy's other business pursuits, he began with a partner who could ostensibly contribute complementary skill. "We tried to start a franchise . . . me and a friend of mine," Randy recounts. "He was a lobbyist for small to medium municipalities, and he would go to DC and lobby for federal money, generally for public works projects. This was when Kentucky Fried Chicken, Wendy's, and a lot of franchises were getting started then. And we were going to franchise the Old Time Picking Parlor." Randy thought he had the promoter he needed. "And the sad part about it was we had like ten or twelve people that were going to combine bluegrass clubs with barbecue places. We were going to franchise primarily with people who already had barbecue restaurants who wanted to put bluegrass in." They developed a plan to sow Picking Parlors all across the Southeast.

But they needed more than a plan; they needed capital, and they struggled to find investors. As a last resort, Randy's lobbyist friend called an acquaintance, Jake Butcher. Butcher was an entrepreneurial banker who had founded the Hamilton Bank chain, based in eastern Tennessee. According to a *Washington Post* profile on him, Butcher was "a local millionaire with a high tolerance for insult and as much brass as he has money" (Conaway 1982). The conversations with Butcher were initially promising. Randy recalls, "We go over to Knoxville, where their corporate offices were. We go up to the penthouse thing, and we meet with him and a couple of his buddies there." Randy then presented his business idea to Butcher. "As soon as he saw it, he said, 'Man, y'all got a gold mine! Count me in. We want to do this with you.'" In hindsight, Randy recognizes there were signs that working with Butcher could be problematic. "He was running for governor, I believe, at the time, so he was generating enemies pretty fast." Randy estimated that he needed about $175,000 to get the franchise concept off the ground. Butcher told Randy the bank would establish a line of credit for $250,000 from which he could draw.

These handshake agreements had to be formalized, though. Randy returned to Knoxville three weeks later to sign papers and start drawing cash. "I won't never forget it," Randy says of the day he went back to Knoxville. "I got up real early to drive to Knoxville, and we get there at the Hamilton Bank building, twelve stories or something, he's in the penthouse. We get up there, and his secretary told us to sit on the couch. So we sit on the couch, waiting. We hadn't got sit down good, and in walk about seven or eight guys, all of them in suits. Walk right on in past us and past the secretary." The secretary immediately protested that these men were charging into Butcher's office uninvited and unescorted. "They don't pay no attention," Randy continues. "It looks like a gangster movie. They just walk right on through the damn door. She's going nuts, and we're trying to figure out what the hell's going on. About five minutes later, they come out and they got Jake in handcuffs. It was FBI agents or Treasury agents, federal people anyway. They just blew right on past her with him. Jake was in handcuffs, and they just walked right out the damn door." Randy claims that Butcher "got sent up on racketeering charges, money laundering," but his more cynical assessment is that "he tee'd off the wrong political people in the state." The bank soon faltered, as did the promises of money that Randy was counting on. "We were that close to being gazillionaires. It was just one of those opportunities we missed, and I didn't have the money to take advantage of it," Randy says sadly. "That was a long ride back from Knoxville that day."

[*Author's note: The facts of this story are difficult to verify. However, the roller-coaster of emotions that Randy experienced were real, and the story is an example of one of the mounting frustrations Randy felt as the Picking Parlor lost its luster.*]

The End of the Picking Parlor

The blows Randy had endured finally took their toll in 1978. Until then, Randy was content running the Picking Parlor, despite its associated stressors. "I fully expected to spend the rest of my life there. I had never even really given a lot of thought to leaving Nashville." But the expensive renovation, the dwindling audiences, and the failed franchise venture were taxing. "Some of the resentment or whatever was building up, but it seemed like everything came to a head at one time," he says. "I think I maybe realized—I just didn't want to admit it—that I was fast burning myself out."

Even the weather was contributing to the strain on Randy. Recalling the winter of 1978, he says, "The temperature never did get above freezing for the whole month of February. And three times during the month we would close the club up; it'd be one or two o'clock in the morning, you'd finally get in bed. By the time you'd get good and warm and start dozing off to sleep, the damn phone would ring. It would be the fire department. I'd have to get up, get dressed, drive all the way back down there, and let them in the damn building and make sure there wasn't a fire because the fire alarm would be going off." Randy says that exceptionally cold weather caused ice to form in the Picking Parlor's sprinkler system. "The least little bit of movement set off that damn alarm," he says. "I had to get up after I was tired and wore out and cold and drive back downtown, let them in, and two of them would walk through the building, make sure there was no fire, and it took a minute and a half. It was just miserable."

The apprentices saw the strain on Randy. "I think Randy was frustrated, because it's really hard to fill the seats in a venue of any kind, let alone every night of the week for five out of seven nights of the week," Chris Camp says. "If you have a nightclub, you got waitresses. You gotta have food. You gotta be serving drinks. You gotta deal with cash flow. You gotta deal with security. You gotta deal with things going wrong all the time. By the time Randy had his fill, he had really taken a beating." Camp recognized Randy was stretching himself thin by operating the three-ring circus of the music store, repair shop, and nightclub. But shedding two of the operations to concentrate on just one of the three would not necessarily have relieved the tension. For example, George Gruhn was focusing on one passion—vintage instruments. Yet even he was subjected to stressful market swings. Camp remembers Gruhn "coming in the Picking Parlor when there was a real lull, and the economic climate was bad, and he said, 'I don't know how I'm going to make it.'"

But the apprentices weren't merely passive observers to the anxious times; they contributed to them. "Randy didn't have the luxury of having a crack team of repair people who were helping him to build the business. Because everyone had their own interests. It was scattering," Chris Camp says. Apprentices earned a portion of the proceeds from any repair work they brought into the shop, so they were incentivized to concentrate on their own success, not necessarily that of the enterprise. Discontent over compensation was brewing among the apprentices. Randy says, "Coley Coleman was my shop foreman. And he was making like 60 or 65 percent—that's what he was getting for what he produced. The rest of them were getting 50 percent. He came in one day and said he was going to have to have more money. He wanted to start drawing 90 percent. There's no way the business can survive doing that." Randy claims Coleman also notified him that the other apprentices were seeking 75 percent. "I had a number of things that had happened that year—cold weather, taxes had gone up. When they came in and demanded that, I told Coley, 'If you think somebody can survive paying those kinds of percentages, then you find the money to buy this place, and I'll see if you can survive doing it.'" Coleman called Randy's bluff.

The Picking Parlor never recovered after the change in ownership from Randy to Coley Coleman. "I financed it," Randy laments. "I think I got $25,000 upfront, which didn't even pay for the damn inventory I had in the place. And it took him almost two years to run it into the ground and bankrupt the place." Chris Camp believes "Randy basically passed the place off from one artist to another, meaning that a businessman did not buy it." But Camp acknowledges, "Randy became incredibly relieved to get out of the Picking Parlor and get out of Nashville, once he got to that point."

The strain also had been clear to Randy's friends for some time. Bobby Wolfe is a fellow luthier who has shared a friendship with Randy going back to Randy's days in Muscle Shoals. "Every time I saw him," Wolfe says, "he was ready to move back South where he could do some fishing."

In later interviews, Randy sanitized his exit story, citing the fatigue of running the business as his primary motivation for leaving. He told one reporter, "A good friend of mine, John D. Loudermilk, a well-known Nashville songwriter, urged me to get out of Nashville. He recognized before I did that Nashville was making me stagnant. He had moved out of Nashville after ten or fifteen years there, and he said he was finally beginning to enjoy country music" (Rhodes 1979). In another interview Randy explained, "We were literally working ourselves to death, trying to run a nightclub and working on instruments. . . . I wasn't able to do much wood work, just trying to hold the business ends together—dealing with the paperwork, accountants, and liquor salesmen. . . . A number of things came to a head, and I finally said that's enough, I want to get back to the coast" (Lowery 2000a). While these are true statements, they do not reveal the frustrated dreams that left Randy disappointed and less resilient to the challenges of running the business. And lurking behind all of these factors was the reality that Randy felt stuck in a rut. He found himself in a position of dreading waking up each morning to go to work. He had violated the promise he had made to himself in Brunswick years earlier.

Today Randy's decision to sell out seems rash, and Randy still harbors some regret. "If I had stayed there, I could have been in pretty good shape now. That damn building would be worth no telling what," he says.

Randy Wood's days of owning one of the hippest spots in Nashville ended abruptly in 1978. He, Irene, and Renee moved back to his native Georgia, where they alighted on Isle of Hope, a quiet, upscale enclave on the coastal marshes near Savannah. Randy's career was far from over at the time, but a significant chapter had reached its conclusion. "Nashville, from my point of view," he confided to the *Savannah Morning News Magazine*, "has served its purpose" (Rhodes 1979).

9

ISLE OF HOPE

It's difficult to tell you are at the workshop of a craftsman with a
worldwide reputation when you enter the dusty, cluttered shop.

———

BOB FLANAGAN of the *Beaufort Gazette*

Nashville quickly receded into the distance in Randy's rearview mirror as
he, Irene, and Renee drove back to his native Georgia in 1978. The business
part of the music business had sapped Randy's energy. "I was so burned
out at that point that I basically became a hermit," he told the *Savannah
Morning News* (Lowery 2000a). "I went almost a year, maybe a little over a
year, that I wouldn't even talk to anybody about mandolins."

He found a home at Isle of Hope, one of several small islands in the
marshes that lie between Savannah and the Atlantic coastline. Isle of
Hope is home to a quiet, upscale residential community, and that suited
Randy perfectly. He only engaged in woodworking on rare occasions,
when he visited the nearby shop of his friend and fellow banjo builder
Harry Lane. "I'd go down and piddle around with him some," Randy says,
"but as far as really actually working, I didn't do anything." He could only
stay away from his passion for so long, though. He soon converted his
garage into a workshop where he planned to work in the sort of quiet soli-
tude he could not find in downtown Nashville.

Although Randy claimed to be a hermit, local newspapers were quick
to showcase the newcomer who had chosen to call their area home. One
article heralded "Local Guitar Maker Known as One of the Best" (Lowery
2000a). After visiting Randy's workshop, Bob Flanagan of the *Beaufort
Gazette* wrote, "It's difficult to tell you are at the workshop of a craftsman

with a worldwide reputation when you enter the dusty, cluttered shop. There are no autographed pictures of the stars.... If Randy likes and trusts you, he might allow you to strum a few chords on a rare instrument that belongs to a music legend, but those are rare occasions" (Flanagan 1982). Like most of Randy's visitors, Flanagan recognized that Randy did not need to impress others to maintain a sense of self-worth.

Randy slowly eased back into commercial lutherie at Isle of Hope. "Wood makes about two mandolins a month, putting about 70 to 80 hours into each instrument," reported Marty Shuter for the *Savannah Morning News* (1996). But Randy's business experience in Nashville had taught him to take a practical approach to making a living as a luthier. He knew which customers could pay the bills. Naturally the newspapers were keen to share with readers the names of country music royalty who played instruments built or repaired by Randy Wood, but Shuter found that "most of Wood's clientele are weekend pickers." Explaining this to *Connect Savannah*, Randy said, "People with day jobs can borrow the money from the bank to buy a custom instrument. Musicians have trouble getting the money" (Sickler 2002). He relished dismantling the illusion that celebrity status goes hand-in-hand with wealth. Randy half-jokingly told *Garden & Gun*, "The pros don't have any money.... My main bread and butter comes from the weekend musicians, because they have jobs" (Moss 2014).

A picture accompanying Don Rhodes's 1979 article in the *Savannah Morning News* shows Randy still sporting impressive sideburns and slicked back hair, Hawaiian shirt buttoned only halfway, and a left front shirt pocket bulging with pens and his six-inch scale. By now, visitors to Randy's workshop could find a "long-haired German Shepherd named Prince, piles of fresh wood shavings, and musical instruments in various stages of repair or construction" (Rhodes 1979). Almost immediately, Randy's shop reached the cluttered state characteristic of his workshops in Nashville.

Frets Magazine Columns

Randy had also become something of a sage after arriving on Isle of Hope. Leaving Nashville crystalized his reputation as an expert in the business of instrument repair—a business he helped create. Roger Siminoff, the editor of *Frets* and a fellow luthier, asked Randy to pen a monthly column on guitar design and construction. In the editor's note for Randy's first column, Siminoff lauds Randy as "among the best-known instrument craftsmen in America" (R. Wood 1979a). Despite the recognition and distinction, Randy was somewhat reluctant to participate. "Siminoff wanted me to write about the innovations of guitars from the seventeen hundreds up to the modern age," Randy explains, "and there's only so much you can say about that." This is a sentiment from someone known for his economy of words.

Nevertheless, he agreed to write for the magazine. The articles are characteristic of Randy's style: there is detail that guitar aficionados can appreciate; there is nostalgia for bygone days of quality and craftsmanship; and there is a sprinkling of humor for good measure.

Randy's first article was nominally about glue and binding, but it became a platform for lamenting the decline in quality of mass-produced instruments. "I think one of the big things back then," he writes about old instruments, "was that people tended to take more time and get a lot closer joints, so that you didn't just fill up a hole with glue. You had the two pieces of wood that you were joining match really well and it didn't have as much of a tendency to come loose" (R. Wood 1979a). He continues to explain how newer instruments not only exhibit lower quality standards but are more difficult to repair:

> Manufacturers have gotten away from designing instruments that can be taken apart. A good example is the binding notch. A lot of the older instruments didn't have the binding overlap the joints like we do today, which made it a lot simpler to take early instruments apart. On most early instruments you could slip a knife underneath the binding and separate the seams. But it's impossible to take a new instrument apart that way, and some of it also has to do with the type of glue they use for the bindings. But overall manufacturing methods are completely different today—quantity seems to be the main thing. Probably needs to be. But I think they could spend a little more time building instruments that would be easier to work on in the future.

Probably the guitars built today are made a little bit bulkier, or a little heavier, because of the manufacturing process and because of the economic pressures that the manufacturers have in the area of warranties. They are having to build instruments that will withstand almost any kind of abuse, whereas years ago they didn't have to do that. I think that is one of the biggest changes in the guitar in the last thirty or forty years. (R. Wood 1979a)

Even though Randy complained about the quality of the new guitars produced by the larger manufacturers, he owed them a debt of gratitude. Had the pre–World War II manufacturing practices continued through the 1970s, the number of instruments in circulation would not have supported a growing population of new musicians. Additionally, any available instruments on the market would likely have been too expensive for many who would be buyers. Instead, a market developed for Randy—a market of players who learned to play on inexpensive instruments and grew to appreciate the vintage quality that Randy has spent his career preserving.

The second article essentially continues his rant from the first, although this time the target is the scope of coatings used to finish the surfaces of guitars:

Since the 1950s and the concurrent introduction of solidbody electric instruments," Randy writes, "the use of ultra-modern lacquers in the form of acrylics, epoxies, and polyesters has become commonplace. I'm sure there must be some advantages in the use of these ultra-modern lacquers; but anyone having to refinish one of these instruments will need, at the very least, a blowtorch and lots of guts to remove the old finish. (R. Wood 1979b)

After penning a few columns, Randy lost steam for writing and whittled away his stash of talking points. "The first few articles I wrote in a couple of hours. Then it started getting harder and harder to dig up the information that was needed." He turned to describing how structural bracing works. In so doing, he revealed one of the signature design features of his guitars:

Over the past five years, I have developed a variation of the standard 'X' bracing system to give more of an overall balance to a flat-top guitar. This is especially noticeable in lead playing and in recorded work. Without the bass 'boom' to contend with, the instrument can be balanced so that all its strings produce a more equal volume. (R. Wood 1979c)

Eventually the well ran dry. "I finally ran out of subjects to write about," Randy says. "I had written about everything that I could come up with. It was taking me a week to dig up the information I needed to write a column that I was getting paid a hundred bucks, or something, for. It wasn't very much. So finally I just had to quit writing it." Randy's time as a columnist was brief, but his few articles were inspirational to fledgling luthiers, including Steve Gilchrist of Australia, who were part of the global audience of *Frets* magazine.

Randy's column in *Frets* was one of several tokens of recognition while he lived on Isle of Hope. His status also was recognized through several honors bestowed on him. He was honored with an exhibit at the Georgia Music Hall of Fame in Macon, Georgia, and in 1984 he was also featured in an exhibit titled "Dixie Frets: Luthiers of the Southeast" at the Hunter Museum of Art in Chattanooga. Of thirty-one luthiers profiled in the exhibit catalog, all except Randy are photographed either working in their shops, holding one of their instruments, or standing in front of their shop. Randy, in contrast, is standing in front of an old pickup truck, petting his enormous Great Dane. Of course, his Hawaiian shirt is untucked over his shorts, and his shirt front pocket is weighed down with pens (Brackner et al. 1994).

Apprentice Scott Kinsey

Despite Randy's attempts to avoid the spotlight, budding guitar builders still sought apprenticeships with him. A 1982 *Beaufort Gazette* article profiled one young, eccentric, and aspiring apprentice named Scott Kinsey. Journalist Bob Flanagan wrote, "On and off for 10 years he was one of Hilton Head Island's favorite saloon musicians.... Always a gentleman and a lady's man, Kinsey could be seen with the island's prettiest girls on his arm—often one on each arm. He knew how to show a gal a good time. He always had a little cash for a bottle of cognac" (Flanagan 1982). But something had inspired Kinsey to leave the nightlife behind: he had found religion in Randy's workshop.

Kinsey's ties to Randy formed before Randy left Nashville. In the early 1970s Kinsey had befriended Bill Godfrey, a Savannahian luthier and friend of Randy's. Godfrey showed Kinsey some basic instrument repair techniques, such as replacing tuners and buffing frets. Kinsey continued to live a bohemian life on Hilton Head, but he reached a point where he knew he needed career traction. "I guess when I was thirty-three, I was working on a sailboat and when I got back, I realized, 'I have got to do something,'" he now says in retrospect. Godfrey told Kinsey he should meet Randy Wood, and he arranged a breakfast where he could introduce them. Recalling the contrast he noticed between Randy and himself at that first meeting, Kinsey says, "In those days, I had really long hair; I had an earring. Randy was a little more conventional than that." He told Randy he would like to apprentice under Randy, but Kinsey recalls that "Randy looked at me, kind of askance, at best. He didn't know anything about me." Kinsey was not able to secure a job, but he did not give up. "I must have pestered Randy for as long as a couple of years, and persistence, I know, means something to him. Finally, I guess he just got tired of listening to me beat on the door. He said, 'All right, all right.'"

Despite years of playing music for a living, Kinsey knew little about lutherie. "When I went in there, literally, I didn't know the difference between a hammer and a jigsaw. I didn't know anything other than I wanted to learn about fixing and making guitars, and I saw a real opportunity there, and he took me in." Kinsey eagerly anticipated his first project, but he learned—as other apprentices before him learned—that the goal of lesson number one with Randy was to learn humility. Kinsey recalls, "He said, 'Here's your first tool,' and he handed me a big shop broom."

Kinsey must have proven his skills with the broom because his responsibilities broadened quickly. The *Beaufort Gazette* reported, "His first day at work, Wood gave him a rare Martin OM-45 to sand. It was worth $8,000!" The article quoted Kinsey saying, "I was scared to death I'd ruin it, but that's the way Randy is. He trusted me not to make a mistake, I guess" (Flanagan 1982).

Randy trusted Kinsey enough to share his hermitage—and his coveted quiet hours—with the young apprentice. "Randy's true working hours were from about 11 p.m. to maybe 4 a.m., because that's when the phone quit ringing. That's when the hangers-on quit coming around. All the things that demanded time, and all the Western movies had been watched. . . . He took me in, and I was with him for a little bit better than four years." Kinsey loved it. "It's a fantasy world here," he told the *Gazette*. "The music, the instruments, the atmosphere in the shop—it's all magic and fantasy" (Flanagan 1982).

The *Beaufort Gazette* noted Kinsey's progress, reporting that "after eight or nine months of learning from the master craftsman, Kinsey is doing most of the repair work at the shop, which frees Wood to build new instruments and fish." Kinsey was part of the fabric of a place that was beginning to mimic GTR and the Old Time Picking Parlor as a place for music fans to gather. "On any given afternoon a small group of bluegrass, country, and folk music pickers will be 'hanging out' at the shop, swapping licks, discussing instruments or playing with the shop dogs, Scooter and Jake" (Flanagan 1982). Randy had, intentionally or unintentionally, turned his home into the favored hangout spot for bluegrass enthusiasts in southeast Georgia.

The article revealed Kinsey's recognition that Randy taught him to solve problems. "According to Randy, most anyone can build a guitar. You can read a set of instructions just like a cookbook. But not all guitar makers are good repairmen. Almost any good repairman is a good guitar maker," Kinsey says. "Randy taught me that when you are confronted with a problem, you study it and figure out five or six ways to go about it. Then you go through each one in your head until you've mentally figured out the best way to tackle the job" (Flanagan 1982). Kinsey credits Randy with sharpening his ability to "use your noodle in a creative way." One day Randy asked Kinsey to glue an instrument back together. "I don't even remember what it was, but it was a very unconventional job," Kinsey recalls. He asked Randy how to do it, but all he got from Randy was a sarcastic "You clamp it." Kinsey had no idea how to begin the job, but he studied it and finally devised a "Rube Goldberg situation," he says. "I ran it by Randy first, before I put glue on it, and I asked, 'What do you think about it?'" Of course, Kinsey wanted to unload some of the burden of responsibility for the outcome of the repair to this expensive piece. "He didn't even look at it; he wouldn't even look up from what he was doing. Randy said, 'Well, is it clamped?' And I said, 'Well, yeah, I think so,' and he just went back to what he was doing and completely ignored me. It's throw-your-ass-in-the-pool, and you're either going to learn how to swim or you're not. I don't know if he did it consciously or not, but he really forced me to learn how to think for myself. Identify a problem, figure out how to solve it, maybe make a trial run, and then do it."

The *Gazette* article acknowledged that the apprentice life was not plush, due to "low pay and sacrifices," but Kinsey looked past the money to put his experience in perspective. "It's been tough. . . . But each day I'm excited about going to work. Randy's not all that generous with praise. He expects the very best quality as routine. Some days I'll think I've done an exceptionally good job on a project, and I'll show it to him. He'll look at it and say that's okay." Kinsey clearly recognized the value of the experience he was earning. "If I stay with it until I've learned this business, then I can walk into any place in the world and say I learned the trade from Randy Wood and they'll know I've worked with the best" (Flanagan 1982).

Notable Instruments: The Phoenix

Even though Randy was no longer working in the heart of Music City, his reputation as a luthier was established. And despite his seclusion on Isle of Hope, his backlog of work grew. In 1995, a New York–based guitar store owner, Joe Pichkur, contacted Randy to make an archtop guitar reminiscent of the ones made by Epiphone in the 1940s and 1950s before the company was absorbed by Gibson. He was so pleased with the result that he wrote an article for *20th Century Guitar* to describe the instrument.

In the article, Pichkur claimed the instrument "has a personality that only can be imparted by Randy himself." The tailstock was hand-cut from brass bell-stock, and "the entire unit is hand engraved with jeweler precision" (Pichkur n.d.). On the fretboard, Randy designed and created cloud inlays inspired by traditional Epiphone designs. He also added an asymmetrical fingerboard extension reminiscent of those found on F-5 mandolins.

Pichkur was most impressed with Randy's internal bracing of the guitar's top. Most archtop guitars were originally designed with two straight top braces running along the length of the top. The braces typically were angled slightly to the guitar's centerline, with the bass side angled more than the treble side, allowing the long-wavelength bass notes more room to resonate on the top. Luthiers later achieved a more balanced tone with braces that cross to form an X. However, the guitars sacrificed response on higher notes in return for the balance. Randy designed a brace pattern for this guitar that is similar to the X-brace designs, but he split the treble bar where it crosses the bass bar. This allowed him to move the treble bar closer to the centerline for better high-frequency response while still maintaining adequate spacing from the neck block at the other end of the brace bar.

Pichkur named this guitar "Phoenix," indicating that it was born from the ashes of the Epiphone inventory that was burned by saddened Epiphone employees after the company was sold to Gibson. He wrote that the Phoenix "is a magical blend of old and new, with memories of a bygone era and old world craftsmanship married to modern design." For Randy, the Phoenix represented yet another job respected and admired by a discerning customer longing for bygone vintage quality.

Notable Instruments: F-12 to F-5 Conversion

Randy found a niche performing what became known as "F-12 to F-5 conversions." Loar-quality F-5 mandolins have long commanded a high price, and many mandolin owners have looked for ways to obtain a mandolin with Loar quality tone without the Loar price tag. Randy found a way to transform Gibson F-12 mandolins into instruments that looked and sounded like the coveted F-5s. Maxwell McCullough wrote about one such conversion for Jay Mireault of Vermont.

The F-12 was introduced by Gibson as a more affordable alternative to the F-5. It sported features requiring less manufacturing time. For example, the F-12 had a squared-end fingerboard instead of a scalloped end. It lacked a pick guard. Its headstock shape was basic, requiring less time to cut than the more intricate shape of the F-5 headstock. Most important, the tops and backs of F-12s were not as painstakingly graduated as the Loar-era F-5s. These design differences lowered the price point of F-12s but compromised the tonal and aesthetic qualities. Gibson produced quite a few F-12 mandolins. While the first production run was short, from 1934 to 1937, the F-12 was reintroduced in 1948 and remained in production until 1980. Some features were improved on the F-12 over time. By 1950, some of the popular F-5 features, including a longer and elevated fingerboard, found their way onto the F-12. As a result, these later models became attractive candidates for F-5 conversions (McCullough n.d.).

This is why Mireault bought a relatively inexpensive Gibson F-12 to send to Randy. "I really liked the feel of the neck of this 1952 F-12 and the slightly wider fretboard. The instrument sounded terrible, however," Mireault told McCullough. Randy's shop was a natural place to send the F-12, because, as McCullough writes, "Randy Wood is one of the most highly respected builders and restorers of mandolins and guitars working today. During his years in Nashville he may have taken apart, studied, rebuilt, and restored more Loars than anyone in the business."

In 1996 Mireault sent his F-12 to Randy. Loar expert Darryl Wolfe contributed a Loar-era pick guard. Mireault also ordered a Monroe era tailpiece and chrome tuning machines. But it was Randy's work that was most transformative. McCullough quotes Mireault explaining:

> He took the instrument apart at the binding, recurved and sanded ("re-graduated") what was a very thick top and back, replaced the tone bars, reworked and bound the headstock, and made a new fingerboard. At my request, the frets were omitted from the fingerboard extension, which is slightly scalloped. Randy also cut and placed the inlay for the headstock and fingerboard, made the bridge, refinished the mandolin, and put all the pieces together. The original Gibson F-12 label was placed back in its original position in the mandolin.

Mireault was proud of his new creation, boasting, "Randy took what was an ordinary appearing and very poor sounding mandolin and brought it to life. The mandolin has the beauty of a Loar period F-5, and the tone is full, rich, well balanced" (McCullough n.d.).

Some collectors spurn such instrument conversions, since the end product is neither an F-5 nor an F-12. Even F-12s now have some value as collectibles. But McCullough acknowledges that as a result of Randy's conversion, "an F-12 that would have gathered dust in an attic is being played and enjoyed on a regular basis." Randy's willingness to perform the conversions underscores his lifelong preference for working to build instruments that musicians want to play rather than instruments that lie mute as collectors' items.

Craftsmanship beyond Instruments

When Randy devoted more time to woodworking at Isle of Hope, he not only focused his attention on musical instruments; he also crafted decorative pieces for yacht enthusiasts and yacht manufacturers. George del Porto, a retired physician in Charleston, South Carolina, owns several instruments that Randy either built or inlaid, but one of the most prized pieces is a table that Randy built for del Porto's sailboat. The table was designed for the cockpit of the boat, with wings that fold for cruising. Del Porto beams with pride when he demonstrates the tightness of the table top joint, the smoothness of its folding, and the inlay of two marlins in the center of the table surface. One newspaper article from Randy's tenure on Isle of Hope observed: "The real irony is in the fact that Randy makes a far greater amount of money from wood work and 'custom pearl work' than from instrument repair and custom work, where his true interest lies. He presently undertakes 'interesting' jobs for yacht and sailboat owners in the Savannah area. He also does all the mother of pearl inlay work for the International Chair Company, which manufacturers 'fighting chairs' for deep sea fishing boats. He does some 'period furniture restoration' and wood sculpturing" (McDonald 1989).

Randy occasionally fielded requests by some well-known customers for nautical projects. Some requests were a bit unconventional. He explains:

A lot of the big sport fisherman got to wanting their things personalized. Some of the big names of manufacturers, like Whaler, Hatteras, a lot of the big yacht makers started ordering chairs with their names

inlaid in them with mother-of-pearl. But then some of the big stars—
I know Jack Nicklaus was one of them—we did them for a lot of golf-
ers and football players. They wanted things personalized. . . . We did
one—some idiot was getting a torpedo launcher. It's just a big board
with rod holders, anywhere from four to six rod holders, which is
mounted on a stanchion, and it sits on the back of a boat, and when
a fish strikes, you can grab a rod. But he wanted two rabbits screwin',
believe it or not. And that was a trip cutting that out of mother-of-
pearl and inlaying that. You run into some of the strangest damn
requests.

The nautical projects brought variety to Randy's work mix, but his reputation remained firmly entrenched in the musical instrument field.

Charlie Daniels's Guitar

It was on Isle of Hope that Randy closed what may have been his longest
open work order in his career. It involved a Martin OOO-18 guitar that
Charlie Daniels had bought at the Picking Parlor. The guitar needed repair, and Randy agreed to fix it for Daniels. However, the repair lost prior-
ity status when Randy's frustrations with the Picking Parlor reached the
critical point.

When Randy left Nashville, he packed Daniels's guitar and moved it to
Isle of Hope, where it sat untouched. Eventually Roger Campbell, Daniels's
lively mustachioed guitar technician, began feeling pressure. Campbell
recalls, "Charlie kept asking me, 'Whatever happened to that old guitar?'"
It did not help that when Campbell called Randy to ask about the guitar,
he found out Randy could not recall where the instrument was, either.

But in 1999, Hurricane Floyd threatened the Georgia coast and spurred
Randy to take action. As the storm approached, Campbell claims that
"the Clinton administration decided to make evacuation mandatory."
Randy had to decide what to take and what to leave, and in the process, he
found Daniels's guitar. Savannah was fortunate to be spared from a direct
hit. Once the threat of the storm passed, Randy committed to repairing
the guitar.

Randy finally presented the repaired guitar to its owner when the Charlie Daniels Band was in the area to play a concert. Daniels was thrilled to finally have the guitar he had wanted for so long. Campbell felt a range of emotions. He was elated to get the guitar back in his boss's hands. He was also awed by Randy's integrity. Given the length of time the guitar went unnoticed, Campbell believes "anybody else would have kept that guitar." Finally, he was grateful for the hurricane evacuation that spurred Randy to finish the job. "Thanks, Bill Clinton, for making that evacuation mandatory!" he exclaims.

Randy's respite on Isle of Hope from 1978 to 2000 gave him the break he needed from his life in Nashville. It restored his desire to build and work on musical instruments. His return to the practice of lutherie also brought increased activity around his shop. It soon became apparent his residential workshop would be inadequate for the growing level of activity he inspired. He needed a new space for his next act, and his Isle of Hope neighbors would make sure he did not forget that.

10

BLOOMINGDALE

*When you walk into Wood's place you can't help
but feel a little magic in the air.*

———

TODD WOOD in *Pooler Magazine*

The night of October 4, 2007, featured a big event for bluegrass fans. The Grand Ole Opry House in Nashville was buzzing with activity in the warm autumn evening, as the International Bluegrass Music Association prepared to kick off the World of Bluegrass convention with its annual awards show. The show is a red carpet, black-tie event that is the bluegrass version of the Academy Awards. It draws everybody who is anybody in bluegrass, including on that night Randy Wood. It was a reunion of sorts for him. A lifetime of devotion to this genre of music had garnered him an Opryland full of friends and musicians whose careers in some way had been shaped by this soft-spoken Georgian. The night was also a validation of Randy's influence, for he was there not as a visitor but as an invited nominee for the Recorded Event of the Year Award. It marked Randy's unlikely return to an active role in bluegrass music promotion, a return that started back at Randy's quiet coastal residence.

The Move to Bloomingdale

Isle of Hope turned out to be too small for Randy. He intended to become a hermit in a peaceful residence with easy access to good fishing, but there is a magnetism about Randy he could not suppress. People were drawn to him and his workshop. The *Savannah Morning News* noted that many of

Randy's musician friends sought him out for a visit or a repair, and "during these visits, jam sessions would inevitably break out," as they always had at Randy's establishments. There was a problem, though. Those musicians "complained they had a hard time finding his islands-area shop" (Walck 2004).

That Randy's shop was hard to find was fine with many of Randy's neighbors. The community began to raise its eyebrows at the growing commercial activity taking place in their quiet suburb. "I lived like a hermit there on Isle of Hope for twenty-two years, working for a few long-time clients from my home," Randy told *Georgia Music*. "But our northern neighbors tend to move down here and try to remake this area into the place they left. I was told because of zoning laws I couldn't run a commercial enterprise, even though it was small, from my home" (Dyer 2011).

So in 1999, Randy and Irene shopped for more space somewhere a little easier to find. "I wanted to find a place where I could get at least five acres," Randy says. "One of the other things I wanted to do was have a place that I could put a small mobile home on, so when my parents got to where they needed to have help, they could live in that and still have their own space, but I'd be close enough to look after them." Randy looked around the outskirts of Savannah for places with available land and decided the small town of Bloomingdale would be his next home. Located west of Savannah, near Interstate 95, Bloomingdale would be much easier for his friends to reach than Isle of Hope. Randy purchased a piece of property by the end of 1999. He soon began building a house and workshop. The Wood family moved to Bloomingdale in the spring of 2000.

But the benefits of Bloomingdale would come at a price—mainly putting up with small-town politics. Randy believed he would have autonomy to buy land and build his home and workshop as he desired. However, some disagreements with the city administration led Randy to realize he would need a business license to operate out of his workshop. While he still did not intend to run a music store full-time, he knew he had to keep a large inventory of spare parts—tuners, strings, guitar bridges, fret wire, and many other items—on hand to effectively repair instruments. A business license would allow him to sell an occasional item if the opportunity arose. That opportunity did arise in the form of a bluegrass renaissance sparked by the critically acclaimed film *O Brother, Where Art Thou?*

The *O Brother* Effect

Randy's move to Bloomingdale was well-timed. A seismic event in bluegrass occurred in December 2000, when the Cohen brothers' film *O Brother, Where Art Thou?* premiered. The film's soundtrack became a runaway success, achieving multiplatinum status. The album featured artists—such as Alison Krauss, Emmylou Harris, Norman Blake, and Ralph Stanley—who had previously been known for country and bluegrass, and it gave them considerable mainstream exposure.

The album received critical acclaim, too. The soundtrack won the Grammy for Album of the Year in 2002. Dan Tyminkski's rendition of "Man of Constant Sorrow" (lip-synched in the film by George Clooney) won Best Collaboration with Vocals, while Ralph Stanley, who had just turned seventy-five two days before the awards show, won the Grammy for Best Male Country Vocal Performance.

The album touched off a new excitement for bluegrass throughout the world. Artists who did not participate in the project still enjoyed the rising tide it produced. Del McCoury, Rhonda Vincent, and Doyle Lawson, among others, reached new audiences in the wake of *O Brother*'s success. And a new generation of musicians were inspired to learn to play acoustic instruments and discover the broader lode of material from which the *O Brother, Where Art Thou?* soundtrack sampled.

Randy Wood Guitars in Bloomingdale

Today, visitors who turn off Highway 80 to Randy Wood Guitars are not simply pulling into a music shop; they are arriving at Randy's compound. Two clusters of buildings dominate the property. To the left, Randy's two-story home, painted white with a large covered front porch where a bench swing invites visitors to relax. A carport and the guest house abut the main house, and large oak trees shade the front yard.

To the right of the driveway is Randy's vocational hangout. The music store has a rustic front, complete with its own porch and rocking chairs. There is even a hitching post between the porch and the parking lot, adding to the old-timey exterior motif. The music shop walls are lined with guitars and photographs from Randy's career. A display case contains several of his mandolins. In the back of the shop, the space opens into a metal building providing additional retail space and the workshop. Every flat surface in the workshop is cluttered. The aromas of sawdust and nitrocellulose lacquer waft through the air. Westerns and old movies usually play on a large flat-screen television mounted on one wall. The opposite wall contains a large window with a view out to the highway. From the outside at night, the window glows with the fluorescent lights from within as Randy works in his most productive hours. "The luthier's woodshop, like Wood's barnlike space off U.S. Highway 80 . . . is as much the artist's studio and showroom as it is a gathering spot for local musicians, bluegrass and country enthusiasts, and neighbors," reports J. C. Gamble in *Savannah Magazine* (2001).

A concert hall occupies the metal building on the work side of the compound. In it, Randy hosts traveling bluegrass bands that perform in the intimate, 100-seat listening room. Local bluegrass fans have been treated to top-rate talent, thanks to Randy's connections. Bluegrass notables including Earl Scruggs, Doyle Lawson, Peter Rowan, and John McEuen have graced the stage of Randy's venue in tiny Bloomingdale, Georgia. As the *Savannah Morning News* explains, "Finding a concert hall that caters to bluegrass musicians outside Nashville is rare. Discovering one outside Savannah—rarer still." The article continues, "While most in the room understand bluegrass isn't for everyone, they do know this: What's happening in Bloomingdale is special and it wouldn't be possible without Randy Wood" (Walck 2004).

Randy eventually achieved what he sought—a home on more land, with a bigger workshop, and an adjacent home for his parents. But getting what he wanted took persistence. So does keeping it. "I've been a thorn in their side ever since," Randy says of his relationship with the Bloomingdale city government since he built his compound. "Every time I sneeze, they run down here to see if I'm doing something illegal."

The Sign

The accusations of illegal activity took the spotlight in local papers shortly after Randy settled onto his property. The questionable offense: erecting a sign. Visitors to Randy's shop find his location marked by a tall sign supported by two legs, one of which is a massive tree trunk. Most visitors have no idea the sign has caused such angst in the small town of Bloomingdale. When Randy built the sign, he had already started leasing space on his property to Dennis Baxter, who operated a small barbecue restaurant on weekends. During the week, Baxter served as the city manager for the neighboring town of Pooler, and he was also Bloomingdale's part-time zoning inspector. He and Randy were friends, and Randy was happy to provide space for Baxter's barbecue stand. For Randy, the food service harkened back to the Picking Parlor days when the nightly music show audiences could dine on pizza served in-house. But when Randy raised the huge sign to advertise his guitar shop and Baxter's barbecue restaurant to drivers on Highway 80, he unwittingly stirred up trouble.

He had good intentions. After the sign was up, he assumed he needed to have it inspected, so he called Baxter to ensure the sign conformed with the permit. Baxter was confused.

"What building permit?" Baxter asked. "You don't need a building permit for a sign."

"I got one . . . well, they sold me one," Randy responded.

"I've never inspected a sign in Bloomingdale."

Randy later confided, "Come to find out, Bloomingdale had been here for almost thirty years, and there had never been a sign permit issued for the city of Bloomingdale until I came here."

Local officials interpreted the rules slightly differently than Baxter did. At a city council meeting, both Randy and Baxter were accused of neglecting the city's rules on outdoor signs. The *Savannah Morning News* had great fun with the irony that Baxter was "responsible for checking violations of the city's 20-page sign ordinance, adopted in October 2002." In a feature article on the squabble, the paper quoted Bloomingdale mayor Ben Rozier declaring, "He's violating the city ordinance by not having a permit. We should get our inspector to take a look at it," referring, of course, to Baxter. Adding to the irony, the article noted that the mayor acknowledged that other nonconforming signs existed in the city, "including one at City Hall itself and another at Bloomingdale's recreation park." Randy was unapologetic. The article stated, "Wood said he believes the sign is attractive and that he doesn't understand why anyone would raise questions about it" (Cochran 2003). The sign still stands today.

The Performance Hall

Despite the acreage and peculiar sign, Randy's place can still prove hard to find. Eddie Adcock, during a performance at Randy's music hall, quipped with the audience, "We don't know how the hell you found it.... We drove by it a couple times" (Walck 2004).

But when music enthusiasts do find it, they find an intimate listening room. Even though it is in a metal building, the concert hall is insulated with sound-absorbing ceiling tiles, wall linings, and carpet. One hundred red padded chairs are packed tightly around a small stage, with old church pews against the left and right walls. The windowless room keeps the audience dark, but a recessed lighting system in the ceiling bathes the stage in warm, bright light for shows. It is a place where the relationship between musician and listener is honored and held sacred. The performers agree. Adcock and his wife, Martha, have been regulars on Randy's stage, and they recognize that Randy's cozy venue brings out a different type of performance than most bluegrass venues. "You have to project in a different way.... We thrive on intimacy here" (Walck 2004). Echoing a sentiment from his days in Nashville, Randy says, "I think people are tired of going to arenas where they need binoculars to see who's on the stage and where they listen to a roar that's supposed to be music" (T. Wood 2009).

The Low-Country All-Stars Sessions

Randy's venue gained wide recognition after he hosted a series of concerts recorded for an album that earned his nomination for the IBMA Recorded Event of the Year in 2007. That event took shape thanks to Randy's longstanding friendship with Vassar Clements. Clements had been spending winters with his cousin Carroll, who lived in Jacksonville, Florida. They frequently made the short drive to the Savannah area to spend time with Randy. "They'd just come up and hang out and pick," Randy says. "I guess the second year that he did that, we were talking about getting some people together to pick, just a jam session. He said, 'You know, we ought to put a band together here and do some shows.'" Randy jumped at the idea. "I'd love to get a band together," Randy told Clements. "Who would you want to get?" Clements immediately suggested Tony Rice, who had been his longtime friend and collaborator. Randy was skeptical. "Tony ain't gon' come down here," he said to Clements. "Hell, I can't afford to pay him, let alone afford to pay you." Vassar coolly responded, "We ain't gon' worry about money. You can count on Rice." Randy knew they would need a mandolin player, and he recommended Tony Williamson. Clements eagerly affirmed Randy's recommendation. They also needed a banjo player. Clements said, "Why don't we check with Scott Vestal? He might be able to do it." Randy called the modern banjo juggernaut who happened to be on break between tours with Sam Bush. Vestal readily agreed to participate.

The last piece to fill was the bass. While Randy was at a workshop in Roanoke, Virginia, he talked with some friends about the group he was putting together. "Somebody who overheard what we were talking about said, 'If you're looking for a bass man who can sing, that guy right over there on the other side of the room is who you need to talk to,'" Randy recounts. The man was Warren Amberson. Randy had not heard him play, but he trusted the recommendation and invited Amberson, who eagerly accepted, thus rounding out the all-star cast.

The group first performed together for a packed house at Randy's hall in late 2004. The show was such a hit with the audience and performers that the group decided to reconvene in December 2005 for a two-night series of shows. After the 2004 concert, Randy knew he had stumbled onto something special. In preparation for the 2005 shows, he hired a Savannah recording engineer, Kevin Rose, to record the event. The result was the *Low-Country All-Star* album. The live recording preserved these masters contributing their inimitable chops to such bluegrass standards as "Salt Creek," "Lonesome Fiddle Blues," and "I Wonder Where You Are Tonight."

The nights were magical. "You could tell just by the way the musicians were getting along. We all knew—even backstage before the show—that it was gonna be a good couple of nights," Randy told *Connect Savannah*, referring to the 2005 shows. "This was essentially a bunch of old friends getting together to do what they love" (Reed 2007). What's more, the intimacy of the venue made the audience an integral part of the show. Front-row patrons were so close to the stage, they had to be careful not to kick the microphone stands. The 2005 recording captured what would be Vassar Clements's final professional recording before he died of cancer.

The bluegrass community recognized the significance of this talent summit, and in 2007 the IBMA nominated the album for Recorded Event of the Year. The winner would be announced at the IBMA's awards show in Nashville. The black-tie affair, which Randy attended with Rose, was a homecoming and validation of Randy's place in the music world. Rose was amazed by the number of connections Randy still had in Nashville. "One thing I learned from this trip," he says, "is Randy pretty much knows every single person in the country music business. And they know him, too! (Laughs) At the special after-party, we met all sorts of major bluegrass people" (Reed 2007).

The award for Recorded Event of the Year ultimately went to the *Double Banjo Bluegrass Spectacular*, which featured Earl Scruggs, Tony Trishka, Bela Fleck, and Scott Vestal. But the event marked Randy's return to prominence as a luthier, music promoter, and social connector—a multifaceted role he had not played since his 1978 departure from Nashville.

Randy Wood's Legacy

Randy Wood will be remembered as a pioneer in the art of repairing the instruments responsible for launching a movement to embrace acoustic music. Pete Kuykendall, the late cofounder of *Bluegrass Unlimited*, recognized that Randy Wood "was one of the first to take older instruments and restore them. He did this at a time when nobody else was even thinking about it" (Lowery 2000). Because he resuscitated these instruments, Randy and those who learned from him saved these works of art from a mute existence. Otherwise, many instruments would have been doomed to collect dust in an attic before the owner's passing might prompt the descendants to trash the instrument with the rest of the unwanted belongings. Luthier and former *Frets* editor Roger Siminoff feels bluegrass music's evolution into a unique genre necessitated instruments that could be adapted for it. He explains:

> For bluegrass music to really work well, it needed to have the instruments and the support of people who could restore old instruments and bring them into a bluegrass music usable form, who could take a tenor banjo out of Dixieland out of the Roaring 20s banjo craze and turn it into a five-string banjo that could be played in bluegrass music in 1965 to 1970.... Randy enabled the growth of bluegrass by being among the group of people who were providing the fuel for the fire.... I'm not taking away from the talented instrumentalists who could play the living daylights out of these instruments. But I don't know if they would have developed the same way if they didn't have the tools.... I just believe that Randy helped fuel that fire and make these instruments available. He made it possible for artists that left his shop to go out and play music because they now had something they could play it with.

Randy proved these masterpieces could be revived and, in the right hands, flourish with tones that new instruments could only hope to imitate.

But Randy has also shown the world that there is hope for new instruments. He was in the vanguard of what is now a thriving industry of luthiers who work not in assembly plants but in cozy workshops producing instruments of timeless quality. "He's the Picasso of acoustic instruments. His art is so defined," engineer Bil VornDick says of Randy's work. He recognizes the "care that has gone into the acoustic characteristics of the wood that he uses." Randy's mandolins and guitars have found their way into the hands of some of the most accomplished players. Mandolinist Mike Compton believes that "Randy's work is second to none. He's right up there with the best." Wayne Henderson, one of today's most highly sought luthiers and a onetime coworker of Randy's at GTR, says, "He's right at the top of builders." The renowned luthier Stephen Gilchrist credits Randy with "helping the revival of quality instrument making." As a young, aspiring mandolin maker in Australia, Gilchrist learned about Randy through

Pickin' Magazine. "I'd comb all those articles, reading every word, trying to absorb that world, which I was so anxious and desperate to become a part of," Gilchrist says. Now that he is among the top echelon of luthiers, he recognizes that Randy's work has produced a "more educated public." That public, which was disheartened by mass-production mediocrity in instruments after World War II, now sees that instrument quality was not doomed to an inevitable downward slide after the days of Lloyd Loar. When instruments such as Randy's early mandolins started raising the bar, the players began demanding better instruments. "It's sort of like a revolving spiral that keeps increasing the quality of the instruments. And it all really started with Randy," Gilchrist claims.

The instruments only represent one side of Randy's legacy, though. Because Randy has been so welcoming wherever he has set up shop, he has—wittingly or unwittingly—provided a place for acoustic music fans to gather. Relationships have formed and communities of musicians have blossomed within the walls of his establishments. At GTR, rehearsal-weary performers found solace simply hanging out among all the vintage guitars hanging on the wall. The Old Time Picking Parlor "was a scene. It was probably the best hang in Nashville," according to VornDick. It was where Charlie Collins helped discover fiddler Mark O'Connor or imbue a sense of the rural roots behind the tunes John McEuen learned growing up in California. The Picking Parlor provided a place where what we would today call "networking" took place to help the careers of musicians, those affiliated with music production (piano tuner Ed Foote, for example), numerous apprentices, and even Randy's shop helper J. T. Gray, who today carries a part of Randy's legacy by preserving the Station Inn as a casual, rustic venue giving fans an intimate setting for listening to their heroes perform. And at Randy Wood Guitars in Bloomingdale, Georgia, visitors on a Saturday can frequently find a bluegrass jam session taking place, with some players driving many miles for the chance to share their passion for playing music with others. All of this is possible because of Randy's remarkable tolerance for humanity that is rooted in a peace about his own life. "I've always wondered why people couldn't do that [be so tolerant of others]. I've always had the notion that if you're content and satisfied with what you do, it doesn't really matter what people think. You have to be content with your own self. Then you can be a lot more pleasant around other people." Many lives have been shaped thanks to Randy's pleasant demeanor stemming from his own sense of contentment.

How does Randy view his legacy? Does he take more pride in the hundreds of instruments and other projects where he has demonstrated his impressive craftsmanship or in the hundreds of people who speak glowingly about the time in their lives when they could hang out with Randy wherever he was plying his trade? "I don't necessarily take more pride in one than the other," he responds. "I think they're both compatible with each other, and the end result is somewhat the same. You hope that what you've done has made people's lives a little easier or more entertaining. Either one of those paths [building instruments or building community], you've had an impact on people's lives, and hopefully for the better."

Back in Nashville at the IBMA awards show in 2007, Randy was far from the rural Georgia farm where he received his first pocket knife and began whittling wood. He was surrounded by crowds of friends, relationships built over a storied career in which he pioneered the art of vintage instrument repair, helped create a thriving vintage instrument market with Tut Taylor and George Gruhn, and operated one of Nashville's most beloved hangouts before retiring and emerging again with a new incubator for acoustic music fans in Georgia. As a result, Randy's fingerprints are everywhere in the acoustic music arena. People are drawn to his personal qualities, to be sure, but that does not fully explain the size of Randy's crowd of admirers. People who spend time with Randy recognize a genuineness that has a timeless resonance amid the fads of the day. Randy's values of honoring musicianship, craftsmanship, and friendship are infectious. And under his humble exterior are layers of fascinating stories from a unique perspective in the music industry—the one who tends to the tools of the trade. Getting to know Randy Wood is a process of continual discovery. Journalist Todd Wood aptly acknowledged the essence of Randy's contribution to the world: "A blend of artful craftsmanship, musical talent, and fellowship—when you walk into Wood's place you can't help but feel a little magic in the air. Surrounded by breathtaking instruments made by Mr. Wood himself—it is hard to believe that a place of this caliber and a man of this great talent is so inconspicuously tucked away in this small Georgia town" (T. Wood 2009). In his workshop, Randy continues to apply his talents to bring joy to people's lives. As he says reflectively, "In the final judgment, that would be what you hope to do."

BIBLIOGRAPHY

Ahrens, Pat J. 2004. "Randy Wood: Luthier." *Bluegrass Unlimited*, November, 48–50.

Brackner, Joey, Bob Gates, Robert Cogswell, Gerry Milnes, and Joe Wilson. 1994. *Dixie Frets: Luthiers of the Southeast*. National Council for the Traditional Arts.

Buckingham, Steve. 1976. "Randy Wood: The Nashville Craftsman." *Pickin'*, June, 18–21.

ClaptonWeb.com. n.d. Accessed January 5, 2019. http://www.claptonweb.com/materiel_acoustiques_en.php.

Coastal Senior. 2002. "Talented Instrument Maker Returned to the Place He Called Home." September.

Cochran, Charles. 2003. "Part-Time Zoning Inspector Fails to Seek Sign Permit." *Savannah Morning News*, November 13.

Conaway, James. 1982. "The Millionaire and the Fair." *Washington Post*, April 11.

Country Western Stars. 1970. "Linda Ronstadt: Sexy New Sweetheart for Country-Western!" *Country Western Stars*, March.

Crossroads Guitar Auction Lot Notes. 2004. http://www.christies.com, accessed January 29, 2012.

Danny Gatton Interview. n.d. https://www.youtube.com/watch?v=678aFBYo9Ck, accessed March 3, 2019.

DeYoung, Bill. 2009. "The Master Craftsman." *Connect Savannah*, July 1.

Dyer, Candice. 2011. "Guitars for the Stars: Randy Wood Cultivates a Not-So-Retiring Retirement." *Georgia Music*, Spring.

Eipper, Laura. 1977. "'Parlor': Back to Bluegrass." *Tennessean*, May 24.

Finney, Pete. n.d. "Will the Circle Be Unbroken—The Nitty Gritty Dirt Band (1972)." Library of Congress. https://www.loc.gov/programs/static/national-recording-preservation-board/documents/WTCBU%20essay.pdf.

Flanagan, Bob. 1982. "Saloon Musician Apprenticed to Master Luthier." *Beaufort Gazette*, August 13.

Forte, Dan. 1976. "Eric Clapton." *Guitar Player*, August, 64–67.

Fuqua, C. S. 2014. *Muscle Shoals: The Hit Capital's Heyday & Beyond*. WindPoem Creative/Cooperative Ink/Fluteflights.

Gamble, J. C. 2001. "Lifelong Luthier." *Savannah Magazine*, March/April, 21–29.

Green, Douglas B. 1976. "Randy Wood's Old Time Pickin' Parlor." *Pickin'*, February, 18–21.

Gruhn, George. 2002. *Gruhn Newsletter #1*. December. http://www.gruhn.com /newsletter/newsltr1.html, accessed March 10, 2011.

———. 2003. *Gruhn Newsletter #11*. October 21. http://www.gruhn.com/newsletter /newsltr11.html, accessed March 10, 2011.

———. 2003. *Gruhn Newsletter #12*. December 13. http://www.gruhn.com/news letter/newsltr12.html, accessed March 10, 2011.

Guitar Aficionado. 2013. "Martin 000-45EC 'Crossroads.'" May/June.

Harvey, Lynn. 1976. "Picking Parlor Builds New Sights & Sounds." *Tennessean*, July 9.

Johnson, Orville. 2011. "In the Middle of Things: Tut Taylor, Heart of the Dobro Community." *Fretboard Journal*, No. 21, 94–108.

Kimsey, Bryan. 1998. "Tony's Guitar." *Flatpicking Guitar*, November/December. http://www.flatpick.com/Pages/Featured_Artist/Tony2.html, accessed January 29, 2012.

Kosser, Michael. 2006. *How Nashville Became Music City, U.S.A.: 50 Years of Music Row*. Milwaukee: Hal Leonard.

Longworth, Mike, Richard Johnston, and Dick Boak. 2008. *Martin Guitars: A History*. New York: Hal Leonard.

Lowery, Don. 2000. "Local Guitar Maker Known as One of the Best." *Savannah Morning News*, January 2, 6D.

Lumpkin, Daniel. 2013. "Master Craftsman: Randy Wood." *American Songwriter*, April 24.

Makos, Jeff. 1996. "Would You Buy a Used Guitar from This Man?" *University of Chicago Magazine*, August.

Malone, Bill C. 1968. *Country Music, U.S.A.: Fifty-Year History*. Austin: University of Texas Press.

———. 2010. *Country Music, U.S.A.* Austin: University of Texas Press.

McCullough, Maxwell. n.d. "Born-Again Mandolin."

McDonald, Janice Brown. 1989. "Randy Wood: Woodworking Wizard." *Bluegrass Unlimited*, May.

Moss, Robert. 2014. "String King: Luthier Randy Wood." *Garden & Gun*, February/March.

Overall, Jim. 1969. "Randy Wood Plies a Unique Trade." *The Picture*, August 30, 10.

Pichkur, Joe. n.d. "Randy Wood's Phoenix." *20th Century Guitar*, 22–24.

Reed, Jim. 2007. "A Nod in Nashville: Local Record Producer Nominated for Live Bluegrass Album of the Year." *Connect Savannah*, October 10.

Rhodes, Don. 1979. "Musical Instrument Craftsman Chooses Savannah as Home Base." *Savannah Morning News Magazine*, September 23.

Rodgers, Patrick. 2006. "Behind the Music: The Instrument Builders of Savannah." *South*, June/July, 78–81.

Rogers, Genevieve. 2007. "Famed Luthier Brings Bluegrass to Bloomingdale." *Spirit Newspapers*, February 15.

Roseberry, J. R. 1998. "Randy Wood Is the Instrument Maker to the Stars." *Savannah Morning News*, September 10.

Rosenberg, Neil V. 1985. *Bluegrass: A History.* Urbana: University of Illinois Press.

Schell, Orville. 1992. *Ferrington Guitars: Featuring the Custom-Made Guitars of Master Luthier Danny Ferrington.* New York: HarperCollins.

Shuter, Marty. 1996. "Savannah Luthiers Honored at Museum." *Savannah Morning News*, September 22.

Sickler, Linda. 2002. "Guitar Man to the Stars." *Connect Savannah*, June 19–25.

Siminoff, Roger. n.d. *Lloyd Allayre Loar, 1886-1943.* http://siminoff.net/loar -background/, accessed March 29, 2017.

St. John, Allen. 2005. *Clapton's Guitar: Watching Wayne Henderson Build the Perfect Instrument.* New York: Free Press.

Stafford, Tim, and Caroline Wright. 2010. *Still Inside: The Tony Rice Story.* Kingsport, TN: Word of Mouth Press.

Stone, Steven. 2008. "Thile's New Loar." *Vintage Guitar*, January. https://www .vintageguitar.com/3456/chris-thile.

Surdoval, Ari. n.d. *Sam Bush, the Gibson Interview.* http://archive.gibson.com /backstage/200606/sambush2.htm.

Walck, Pamela E. 2004. "Lowcountry Lonesome." *Savannah Morning News*, February 13, 5V.

Wolfe, Darryl G. 1987, 1993, 1999, 2001. *F-5 Journal.* Aiken, SC: Darryl G. Wolfe.

Wood, Randy. 1979a. "Randy Wood on Guitars: Guitar Evolution." *Frets Magazine*, October, 44.

———. 1979b. "Randy Wood on Guitars: Instrument Finishes." *Frets Magazine*, November, 48.

———. 1979c. "Randy Wood on Guitars: Top Bracing." *Frets Magazine*, December, 51.

———. 1980. "Randy Wood on Guitars: Braces and Tone Bars." *Frets Magazine*, January, 45.

———. 1980. "Randy Wood on Guitars: Scalloped Bracing." *Frets Magazine*, February, 68.

———. 1980. "Randy Wood on Guitars: Truss Rod Tips." *Frets Magazine*, April, 58.

———. 1980. "Randy Wood on Guitars: Binding: Why and How." *Frets Magazine*, August, 46.

Wood, Todd. 2009. "All from a Block of Wood." *Pooler Magazine*, July/August.

BIBLIOGRAPHY

INTERVIEWS BY DANIEL WILE

Ahrens, Pat, November 14 and 21, 2010. Not Cited (NC).

Burch, Curtis, December 29, 2011. NC.

Camp, Chris, February 19, 2012.

Campbell, Roger, November 12, 2011.

Collins, Charlie, November 11, 2011.

Compton, Mike, October 9, 2017.

Ferrington, Danny, June 12, 2011.

Foote, Ed, April 22, 2011.

Gilchrist, Steve, November 30, 2017.

Gray, J. T., December 30, 2011.

Gruhn, George, interview by Daniel Wile and Dennis Satterlee. February 4, 2011.

Hedgecoth, John, December 28, 2011.

Henderson, Wayne, February 3, 2012.

Henry, Red, November 15, 2010.

Huffmaster, Raymond, December 29, 2014. NC.

Kinsey, Scott, April 22, 2011.

McEuen, John, September 13, 2012.

Siminoff, Roger, January 4, 2017.

Sloan, J. D., May 24, 2011. NC.

Taylor, Tut, May 19, 2011.

VornDick, Bil, June 2, 2011.

White, Buck, June 2, 2011.

White, Roland, November 27, 2010.

Williamson, Tony, and Randy Wood, November 7, 2010.

Wolfe, Bobby, and Darryl Wolfe, April 1, 2011.

BIBLIOGRAPHY

Wood, Randy, November 8, 16, 22, 2010.

Wood, Randy, January 4, 2011.

Wood, Randy, January 16, 2011.

Wood, Randy, January 25, 2011.

Wood, Randy, January 26, 2011.

Wood, Randy, March 1, 2011.

Wood, Randy, March 13, 2011.

Wood, Randy, May 27, 2011.

Wood, Randy, June 6, 2011.

Wood, Randy, June 17, 2011.

Wood, Randy, September 18, 2011.

Wood, Randy, May 21, 2013.

Wood, Randy, January 19, 2019.

Wood, Randy, March 23, 2019.

INDEX

Page numbers in **boldface** refer to illustrations.